• •

LIBERATE YOUR CHILD'S LEARNING PATTERNS

• •

Liberate Your Child's Learning Patterns

BY
PRISCILLA L. VAIL, M.A.T.

Adapted for parents from
Learning Styles: Food for Thought and 130 Practical Tips for Teachers K-4

SIMON & SCHUSTER
New York London Toronto Sydney Singapore

Books by Priscilla L. Vail, M.A.T.

Seize the Meaning!
*Help Your Child Move from Learning
to Read to Reading to Learn*
(Kaplan Publishing, 2002).

Homework Heroes, Grades K-2:
It's a Bird. It's a Plane. It's Done
(with Drew and Cynthia Johnson,
Kaplan Publishing, 2001).

Homework Heroes, Grades 3-5:
It's a Bird. It's a Plane. It's Done
(with Drew and Cynthia Johnson,
Kaplan Publishing, 2001).

Homework Heroes, Grades 6-8:
It's a Bird. It's a Plane. It's Done
(with Drew and Cynthia Johnson,
Kaplan Publishing, 2001).

Reading Comprehension:
Students' Needs and Teachers' Tools
(Modern Learning Press, 1999).

Language Assessment for Grades 3 & 4
(Modern Learning Press, 1998).

A Language Yardstick:
Understanding and Assessment
(Modern Learning Press, 1997).

"Words Fail Me":
*How Language Works and What Happens
When It Doesn't*
(Modern Learning Press, 1996).

Emotion:
The On/Off Switch for Learning
(Modern Learning Press, 1994).

Learning Styles:
*Food for Thought and 130 Practical Tips
for Teachers K-4*
(Modern Learning Press, 1992).

Common Ground:
*Whole Language and Phonics
Working Together*
(Modern Learning Press, 1991).

About Dyslexia:
Unraveling the Myth
(Modern Learning Press, 1990).

Smart Kids with School Problems:
Things to Know and Ways to Help
(NAL Plume Paperback, 1989).

Gifted, Precocious, or Just Plain Smart
(Modern Learning Press, 1987).

Clear & Lively Writing:
Language Games and Activities for Everyone
(Walker & Co., 1981).

The World of the Gifted Child
(Walker & Co., 1979).

Kaplan Publishing
Published by Simon & Schuster, Inc.
1230 Avenue of the Americas
New York, NY 10020

For bulk sales to schools, colleges, and universities, please contact: Order
Department, Simon & Schuster, Inc., 100 Front Street, Riverside, NJ 08075.
Phone: (800) 223-2336. Fax: (800) 943-9831.

For information regarding special discounts for other bulk purchases,
please contact Simon & Schuster Special Sales at 1-800-456-6798 or
business@simonandschuster.com

Cover Design by Cheung Tai
Book Design by Lili Schwartz
Editor: Beth Grupper

Manufactured in the United States of America
September 2002
10 9 8 7 6 5 4 3 2 1
Library of Congress Cataloging-in-Publication Data

ISBN: 0-7432-3051-5

CONTENTS

THE RATIONALE

This book is about learning patterns, children, teachers, curriculum, classroom dynamics . . . and you.

First things first. Learning patterns? What does that mean? Each person has patterns of strengths and weaknesses, clusters of likes and dislikes, and although the particulars may change from time to time, the underlying structures remain consistent. In recognizing learning patterns, we see *how* different people learn, what personal energies they tap in the learning process, and the ways in which they absorb information and internalize new concepts.

Most people's underlying learning patterns are unique and permanent, they transcend socio-economic lines, and are not measurements of intelligence. However, from such mechanical difficulties as allergies to such complex situations as divorce, in many instances we can minimize negative patterns with skillful structuring. Similarly, we can reinforce the positive patterns. Whether the patterns are positive or negative, temporary or permanent, they need to be addressed.

What role do you play? By learning to recognize and understand your child's unique learning patterns, you can create optimal learning settings at home. You can help your child apply his own natural strengths to academic tasks and to the real life learning that brings joy and sparks interest.

This book is different from the many articles and books on this subject whose focus predominantly links learning patterns with learning disabilities (LD). While some learning patterns compromise a child's ability to succeed in a regular classroom, others are easy for teachers to accommodate, and they make life more interesting for everyone. And just as students have different learning patterns, teachers have distinctive teaching patterns. Enlightened teachers who understand different ways of learning, and who are aware of their own teaching preferences, can use an imaginative selection of methods and materials to help an average learning-abled student become a learning-enabled success. As a parent, you play an important part in making this happen. By bringing your child's learning patterns to the attention of his teachers, you can help ensure that there are opportunities for him (and other children like him) to incorporate his strengths in the classroom setting. Throughout the book you'll find suggestions to communicate information to your child's teachers.

Intellectual appetite is the phrase that pops to mind, and the parallels with school seem limitless: active cooks and active learners; physical hunger and intellectual appetite; parents and keepers of classrooms, coordinating their efforts; bodily nourishment and food for intellectual growth; commonness of purpose and variety of approach. Variety is the spice of life, and obviously a good blend sets the stage for success.

Our family kitchen makes a tasty metaphor. Just last week, our usually far-flung entire family of three grown daughters, two husbands, our son in his mid-twenties, six grandchildren, along with me and my husband, were together for a long weekend. Everyone was excited to see everyone else, to laugh, compare notes, reminisce, and to hang out around the large dining room table. Cooperative (perhaps well-raised, says the grandmother), each one offered to help with the cooking.

One child is what I would call a sprawler. She gets out every sort and type of ingredient, utensil, and equipment she could possibly need before she begins. It seems that the entire length of highway I-95 would hardly be enough counter space for her.

The next child is what I would call a compartmentalizer. Before beginning, she checks the cupboards and refrigerator to be sure all ingredients are on hand, checks the pot locker for what she'll need, and, taking out only what is required for the first step, she starts the recipe. When finished with those items, she puts them back in place, washes whatever bowls or pans she has used, and proceeds to the next step. Her complicated and delicious treats come from a perpetually orderly laboratory.

Inventor and mad scientist are appropriate designations for the third child. She flings open the doors of the pantry shelves and refrigerator, stands back, hums, and begins to create. She seems to make it all up as she goes along, using her senses of smell and sight to tickle our sense of taste. Her nose is more important to her than the recipe book, and her eye takes inspiration from looking over possible additions or variations.

Next comes the one I would call the biggest-bang-for-the-buck whipper-upper. Knowing exactly which canned and frozen items to combine with something fresh, this cook likes minimum preparation, maximum relaxation, and a tasty result.

Then we have the one I would call Flash in the Pan: Quick ideas that sometimes hit the bull's-eye, but often don't taste very good.

Each has the same goal: nutritious and enjoyable food. But the approaches couldn't be more different. So, considering the setting, the emotional expectation level for the weekend, and the different approaches (which work well in each person's home kitchen but overlap or interfere in shared space), we were loaded with spat potential. How fortunate that, without any "tactful suggestions" from the grandmother (whose teacher persona sometimes arrives uninvited), they sorted out ahead of time who would be responsible for which part of the meal, and elected all noncooks to the cleanup crew.

As we enjoyed the fruits of various labors, I was also amused to notice the different ways grandchildren eat. One child goes for the Calvinist New Englander approach: eat the obligatory stuff first, and save the best for the last. A cousin just his age does the opposite. Operating on the pleasure principle, he tucks into the best while his appetite is the sharpest, and then fills in around the edges afterwards. One little girl, who likes tidy hair and clean hands, mushes everything around together until it's like a casserole. The Tomboy with scabs on her knees keeps all categories widely separated. If her mashed potatoes touch the salad dressing, she considers them contaminated and won't eat them, even though she will eat the salad and ask for seconds. Another child simply picks. All have different ways of ingesting the same offerings.

Similarly, children have different patterns, preferences—or occasionally—foibles in regard to learning. Your child's teachers cannot individualize the curriculum for each student, nor should they, any more than the family cook should prepare a separate menu for each person. It's unrealistic. And, in typical contemporary classrooms—where mainstreaming, increased cultural diversity, ballooning class sizes, and a wide range of behavioral attitudes are the norm—it's impossible. Furthermore, some of the most permanent and exciting learning takes place as children bounce ideas off one another in group discussion of a common question or concept. What does matter, and matter vitally, is that your child's teachers present ideas and materials in a variety of ways so as to match the learning patterns—or intellectual appetites and preferences—of your child and his classmates. Your child, regardless of how he learns, must be allowed to flourish in the classroom.

We will look at six learning patterns and the issues they generate. The choices come from an expansion of the standard, stereotypical, predictable list generally associated with LD, to a more multidimensional set of categories drawn from the research on talent, competence, and success, as well as difficulty. This, then, is a novel amalgam, and one that embraces the different kinds of learners who have peopled my classes. Experienced teachers have met trainloads of students who fit these six descriptions singly or together. In fact, your child's classroom includes students with each of these patterns.

In the first part of this book, "Which Learning Patterns?" we will follow a format: look at each learning pattern, see why it matters, and how it puts children "at promise" or "at risk." While your child's education takes place both inside and outside of the classroom, the focus in this section will be on the impact of each learning pattern in the classroom. Once you know how your child's style manifests itself at school, you will have a better sense of what to focus on at home.

The second part, "Addressing Learning Patterns, Meeting Needs, and Having Fun," begins with the twenty-two Principles of Good Practice applicable to all grades. Then, for each grade level from kindergarten through fourth grade, we will:

- anticipate the major focus of the curriculum, so you know what to expect as your child advances from grade to grade, and see the opportunities and pitfalls for each learning style;
- offer at least three home activities for each of the six patterns at each grade level: 120 total, plus the 22 Principles of Good Practice, for a grand total of 142.

The afterword is followed by three appendices containing a reprint of an article summarizing the current information on ADD/ADHD, the Dolch Basic Sight Word List, and additional resources for those who wish, or need, to explore in greater depth.

PART 1

WHICH LEARNING PATTERNS?

Since people are multifaceted, each person has more than one way of learning. But most of us have predominant clusters, preferred channels, and secondary, subordinate approaches. As you look at the following list, remember not to restrict your view of your child to only one pattern.

In looking for patterns, we ask:

1. Is your child *available for schoolwork:* physically, emotionally, intellectually?

2. Does your child learn best through *three-dimensional or two-dimensional* materials?

3. Is your child predominantly a *simultaneous or sequential* processor?

4. Does your child learn best with *multisensory* teaching: visual, auditory, kinesthetic/tactile?

5. Is your child *eager to make connections:* filing, retrieving, recombining?

6. Is your child either *gifted, precocious, or just plain smart:* in factual, aesthetic, or imaginary realms?

ADD/ADHD (Attention Deficit Disorder, Attention Disorder with Hyperactivity) would often be included in this type of list.

But because so many questions about this syndrome remain unanswered, and so much available information is self-contradictory, I chose not to include the topic here. Instead, I have reprinted in appendix A an article with general descriptive and cautionary comments from five physicians who, in addition to their medical practices, are active in education.

CHAPTER 1

AVAILABLE FOR SCHOOLWORK

- physically
- emotionally
- intellectually

What This Learning Pattern Is and Why It Matters

To be available for schoolwork, a child needs to marshal energies, focus interest, and distribute attention. Together these make up what is called "executive function." In training her residents in neurology, Martha Denckla, M.D., explains executive function by using the acronym ISIS, which stands for the four abilities to:

Initiate an action,

Sustain attention,

Inhibit distraction,

Shift focus.

The subsets of executive function relate intimately to three types of availability. You need to assess whether your child is available for schoolwork physically, emotionally, and intellectually. If your child is unavailable, no matter how fascinating the teacher or engaging the subject matter, learning will not take place. Even though these absences may be transitory, they need to be acknowledged and addressed for forward motion to occur.

Physically Available

The physically available child can reason, remember, concentrate, listen, carry out instructions, maintain eye contact, and last but far from least, have enough energy left for humor.

How can a child be sitting in a classroom yet not be physically available?

Weary children aren't available for the active exploration of real learning. Many children today stay up late listening to music or watching TV or videos in their bedrooms. Others stay up late to have after-work time with their parent(s), and some children just have an unmet need for more sleep than their peers require.

Hungry children who have skipped breakfast lack the fuel to sustain effort in learning.

Physical sensations of visual and auditory awareness add extra dimensions to what we know of the world, but they also cause interruptions in availability. Many children have trouble filtering out such externals as auditory or visual distraction, or ignoring the internal itch of daydreaming.

(For example, as I write this, I am sitting on an airplane in front of two people in the throes of making friends. They are trading jokes and personal histories. He preens with his voice, she admires with a high giggle, and I cannot read. Their voices drown out the *sounds* of the words on the page, and I cannot write. Their words intrude on my powers of word selection, and I can't say what I mean. I guess I'll give in and get out my embroidery.)

The child with a history of middle-ear infections may have an undetected hearing problem leading to observable but misunderstood trouble with concentration, following directions, and participating in the give and take of group discussion. For obvious reasons, the same comments apply to children with allergies.

Other children are unintentionally drawn to visual stimuli: a visitor entering the room, people passing by on the street outside, patterns of clouds, or patterns of floor or ceiling tile, not to mention the hypnotism of a Day-Glo barrette on the girl three rows ahead, or the surprise of a wastebasket moved to an unaccustomed place.

A Child "At Promise"

Stefan and his body are good friends. Although he is only six, he can kick a soccer ball with either foot, score a run playing tennis-baseball on the lawn with his older cousins, and draw or color with skill. What he does with his feet and his hands satisfies his mind and his heart.

His body sits comfortably in a chair, his posture is relaxed in class, and he holds his pencil comfortably, moving it across the lines with age-appropriate skill and rhythm. He is as pleased with his learning as his teacher is with her teaching.

A Child "At Risk"

Mark's parents live in the biggest house on their hill. They are both busy professionals who provide unlimited material comfort. For Mark's tenth birthday, they gave him his first wish: an electronic center for his bedroom. It contained a stereo, radio, tape deck, CD player, TV with a big screen, and a VCR.

Unless they are traveling, Mark's parents come home after work, check in, change their clothes, and check out again, leaving Mark in the care of a domestic servant whose nightly TV schedule is mapped out well in advance. She doesn't care what time the boy goes to sleep as long as he is in his room. He often stays up until midnight.

Mark suffers from a bad case of what the Jung Institute has labeled "affluenza."

Emotionally Available

The intact child with positive self-concept who comes to school rested, fed, disease- and allergy-free, who has at least one good friend, and whose parents (or parent) value education and learning, is available for learning. The child who has experienced this combination develops an appetite for purposeful sensations and learns to arrange internal and external structures that invite and protect energy, interest, and attention. Such children are usually able to choose projects that are likely to succeed and that fit in the realities of domestic time and space. It is as though they set themselves up for success.

Many of today's children are frightened by mystery or violence at home, or are bereft at the departure of a separating parent, or are confused by yo-yo-ing custody plans, or mourn the death of a family member or pet. These children bring with them to school pangs of wistfulness and yearning that spirit away availability on the wings of sadness.

The child who has tasted school failure frequently enough to anticipate future disappointment, the kid abandoned by lost friendship, the child with a guilty conscience, or the depressed child cannot focus on such externals as classroom attention. These negative experiences disrupt the availability of increasing numbers of children each succeeding year as our society changes.

Some experiences—such as disruptions in friendships—are common childhood events, but commonness doesn't diminish pain. Others—like emotional disturbance over parental separation—exert influences that adults tend to minimize or overlook completely. For example, guilty consciences often trouble young children of separation or divorce: "If I had been better . . .", "I yelled at my dad and then he moved out . . ."

Psychiatrists tell us that the incidence of clinical depression in childhood is seriously underdiagnosed. The depressed child is simply not available for learning.

A Child "At Promise"

Helen has mild learning disabilities. She is prone to reverse her letters and numerals, her spelling breaks down when she is under pressure, and her ideas come so quickly she sometimes has trouble writing them down. Merry, sometimes naughty, she has a friend in every grade, is a skillful athlete, and her artwork is joyously colorful.

When she thinks about school, she thinks first about her friends and last about academic challenge. A sixth grader now, she has always done well when she had a warm relationship with her teacher. Her history exemplifies the maxim that kids move from "learning to love to loving to learn."

A Child "At Risk"

Sarah didn't want to tell about her parents' separation in school. Without knowing why exactly, she took the blame. Furthermore, she felt embarrassed. Because she herself didn't quite know what to make of the situation, she didn't know how to explain it, defend it, or despair over it to others.

Often when the teacher was explaining something, Sarah's mind would drift off to remember the smell of her father's shirt when he undid the paper ribbon from the laundry, shook it out, put it on, and buttoned it. She loved to kiss him then, smelling the magical combination of cotton, ironing, and him.

Now, he comes to their apartment every other week for his "share of the custody." That means her mom goes away to stay at Aunt Barbara's. *Who do I love? Which do I love? Who loves me?* drown out the sound of her teacher's voice, until that comes through to her in anger. "Sarah! Pay attention!"

Intellectually Available

Emotion and intellect support one another. The emotional brain (the limbic system) interprets incoming stimuli and then sends its interpretation as if by loudspeaker to the rest of the brain. When the emotional brain notices a stimulus, the sound of a school bell for instance, it decides whether the stimulus is humdrum, or threatening, or appealing. If a danger message is broadcast, the gears of memory and reasoning lock. If a message of interesting excitement comes through, pathways to memory clear, new ideas burst forth, and associations blossom.

Paradoxically, the child who feels safe is the one who dares take intellectual risk. Children in a classroom that offers both safety and exploration are intellectually available. The emotional climate of the classroom is totally and directly under the control of the teacher. It is a point of view, not a point of purchase. The same thing is true at home. The emotional climate of your home—and, consequently, your child's willingness to take intellectual risks—is totally and directly under your control.

Intellectual availability expands through overall intelligence, adequate language development, and the use of methods and materials designed to capture children rather than to make them obedient.

A Child "At Promise"

"I can't wait to get into here," said second grader Flora to the librarian. "My grandparents are going on a trip to those places you see about on the news, but I can't tell where they are on the globe. And, I want to find out about those beautiful designs they have on their clothes, and I want to read some stories about kids in Lapland and Russia, and if my grandparents bring me back some hats and parts of costumes, me and Kendrosha and Maria are going to make an exhibit. I've never heard of most of this stuff before. I can't wait! Will you help me with the globe, and finding the stories?"

A Child "At Risk"

Jeremy is a twelve-year-old boy whose scores on aptitude tests confirm his teachers' and parents' hunch that he is smart. But Jeremy's motto is Safety First. He puts pressure on himself to maintain his record of high marks, tidy papers, and correct answers.

In third grade, his teacher was a free spirit who preferred open-ended questions to ones with correct answers in the back of the book. It was Jeremy's unhappiest academic time. The teacher's favorite questions were, "What do you think?" and "What might come next?" Jeremy's consistent query, "Is this right?" was met with "How can you find out?"

CHAPTER 2

THREE-DIMENSIONAL OR TWO-DIMENSIONAL

What This Learning Pattern Is and Why It Matters

Research from neurology tells us that many people with great potential or power in the three-dimensional sphere have parallel difficulty with two-dimensional tasks. The 3-D spheres include science, engineering, mathematics, medicine, architecture, drama, athletics, and politics, not to mention construction and mechanics. The 2-D realm uses the abstractions of words and printed symbols with no intrinsic meaning of their own. There is no logic that says a squiggle like *s* should make the sound /s/.

When they start school, children confront symbols in every corner of the classroom: letters, whole words, numerals, process signs for arithmetic. The child with strong two-dimensional capacities absorbs them easily, learning from print. Without the kind of appropriate training we will see in the section on multisensory learning, the three-dimensional learner, frequently highly intelligent, is confused or lost.

The ratio of children's 3-D/2-D power influences the success or failure of their early school years, distinctly coloring their view of themselves as learners, which in their own interpretation, determines whether they are worthy or unworthy—lovable or despicable—human beings. Children judge themselves harshly, being more forgiving of their puppies than they are of themselves.

A Child "At Promise"

First grader Noah loves to build with blocks, swing from trapezes on the playground, wear hats and capes at "Act It Out" time. He has been a story maven from early childhood, seizing on letters and words as keys to the kingdom of imagination and thought. 3-D/2-D? He's got it together.

A Child "At Risk"

Zeb (short for Zebulon) is Noah's brother, older by eighteen months. Zeb didn't start talking until after Noah had begun. His parents rationalized that he just hadn't used words earlier because he hadn't needed them. They had anticipated and met his needs. Then, they reasoned, when Noah started to talk, Zeb scrambled to catch up. Unfortunately, things aren't that simple. Zeb's language is intrinsically weak.

Although the class he originally belonged to is in third grade now, he is in second grade. His teachers use the phrase "the gift of time." His parents say, "We left him back." The decision was based on the hope that an extra year would let Zeb close the language gap, and that the brothers would enjoy being together in the same class.

Zeb's second-grade teacher is particularly skilled in origami, the art of paper folding. Because she wanted to give him some individual attention and a boost to his self-esteem as he headed into second grade for the second time (and with his younger brother), she showed him five of the introductory steps of paper folding. This boy, whose spelling was backward and inside out—and whose handwriting sprawled on the page—learned, used, and extended the introductory origami lesson into the ability to make first a butterfly, then a parasol, and finally a cube.

Zeb's 3-D sense guides his fingers to remarkable achievement, admiration from his peers, and well-earned pride. But his problems with both spoken and written language remain and will not melt away spontaneously.

CHAPTER 3

SIMULTANEOUS OR SEQUENTIAL

What This Learning Pattern Is and Why It Matters

The world is made up of both pyramid builders and parachute jumpers. Sometimes, they are called assemblers and recognizers.

The sequential thinker is happy starting with empty space, gathering a few conceptual blocks, assembling them into a sensible conceptual platform, and then layering on increments, finally attaining a pinnacle from which to call "a-ha!" This is a bottom-to-top learner, a pyramid builder, an assembler.

The simultaneous thinker works in the opposite direction. Starting with a global concept—having the whole picture in mind—this person works down layer by layer or bit by bit, seeing the internal nuts and bolts of the structure whose outlines he already understands. This is a top-to-bottom learner, a parachute jumper, a recognizer. He calls out "Eureka!" at the beginning of his work.

Why does this matter? Neither pattern is more or less noble, but discomfort with one approach or the other can hobble an otherwise successful learner. Kids chafe at presentations that move in the wrong direction. When there is a conflict between teaching and learning preferences in this domain, friends become enemies, misunderstandings flourish, and learning withers.

The academic deck is stacked against the global learner—the parachute jumper—in this way: Roughly 70 percent to 80 percent of the material used in classrooms are designed by and for sequential processors—pyramid builders. In a later section, we will see some simple ways to accommodate both patterns. If your child is a parachute jumper, bringing these options to the attention of your child's teacher might help. For now, let's meet some children.

A Child "At Promise"

"Stop! I spent $18.95 on that model. Read the directions before you begin!"

Too late. The pieces were dumped across the table, the bones of a battleship scattered in random pattern and glorious disarray.

Eight-year-old Jason—a "Eureka!" man—was like a legitimate wizard: He saw the overall design, its components, and the sequence needed to put them together. Working with both hands, and only occasionally checking the picture on the box, whistling as he worked, he produced a perfect finished product. And there wasn't a single piece left over.

A Child "At Risk"

Pamela is an orderly second-grade girl. Her shirt stays tucked in. Even though she runs and plays happily on the playground, joining in whatever game is going on, she is seldom mud-splattered. She takes great pride in the artistic quality of her written work; her reading and spelling are the reliable harvest of a strong multisensory phonics program. She is at risk.

Why? She is a methodical child who works at a measured pace. Intuitive leaps make her uncomfortable. She likes and needs to size up things carefully ahead of time. Her deliberate ways seem pedantic to her teachers, other kids' parents, and sometimes other kids. She was misunderstood by last year's teacher, who said, "Pamela is a slow thinker." This implies dim-wittedness, yet this child is very intelligent. She chooses her words with care and precision, arranges her thoughts in orderly progression, and uses them effectively to develop complicated concepts.

CHAPTER 4

MULTISENSORY LEARNING

- visual
- auditory
- kinesthetic/tactile

What This Learning Pattern Is and Why It Matters

Increased knowledge has helped us move beyond the simplistic temptation to call Ned a "visual learner" or to say "Samantha just isn't an 'auditory learner.'" Research on learning teaches us that learners of all ages use combinations of these patterns and may vary the recipe according to the situation. Most of us need to harness all three when tackling unfamiliar tasks.

I think of the highly accomplished college student who takes notes in lectures or while reading: "I almost never need to review them," she said. "When I want to remember something, I can see it in my mind's eye. I know just where it is on the page. But if I didn't take notes, I'd just float along on the general ideas, listening to the professor's voice, looking at his slides. I'd have a lovely time, but I wouldn't have an anchor."

Most of us are probably the same. Multisensory teaching and learning, in which we are hearing *and* seeing *and* using our hands, helps us harness intelligence (and availability) to the opportunity at hand.

That said, it is also true that many learners have a discernible strength or weakness. One pathway is stronger or more reliable than the others. Having considered the three together, let's look at them separately.

Visual Learning

The visual system ferries images that the brain then registers, interprets, and sometimes stores in memory. (While 20/20 vision is handy, problems in the mechanical aspect of vision can be helped with glasses or contact lenses.) We need to pay attention to both interpretation of—and memory for—visual stimuli.

Fortunate children are born with a metaphoric mental photocopier, a machine with smooth, unwrinkled paper, a goodly supply of high-visibility ink, and a strong enough light to read images boldly. The on/off switch is reliable.

Other children, intelligent and eager to do well, seem to have a photocopier from a lemon batch: The images are blurry or reversed, sometimes they fade out quickly. For these kids, the attempt to learn sight words or individual letters is an exercise of conjuring in reverse: Now you see it, now you don't. Vanishing acts turn learning into a game of smoke and mirrors, leading first to uncertainty, then to self-doubt.

Difficulties in this area, which obviously undermine reading skills, are sometimes called dyslexia. It is important to remember, though, that dyslexia has more than one manifestation. It may cause trouble in listening and organizing, as well as in reading and writing.

A Child "At Promise"

Susannah's teacher showed her a list of the *wh* words (*who, what, when, where, why, how*), explaining to her which was which and offering some simple clues for telling them apart. The child was able to look, learn, remember, and distinguish them quickly and accurately. Developing and using clues will stand her in good stead all the way through school, as she learns foreign language vocabulary, chemistry symbols, or simply the process signs for arithmetic and mathematics.

Her good fortune happens to come hand in hand with being very intelligent, but an effective or marginal mental photocopier isn't the equivalent of high or low intelligence. Reliable machinery is a convenience, not a merit badge.

A Child "At Risk"

No matter how hard Benjy tried, no matter how interested he was in the story, and no matter how much he admired the illustrations in the whole-language materials[1] his teacher was using successfully with many other children in first grade, he couldn't remember the words from the story when he saw them in other contexts. Flashcards didn't work. Bribes didn't work. Scolding didn't work. Good attitude had no corrective effect.

Benjy is a highly intelligent boy, curious, active, a natural athlete—and a boy who can build complicated and beautiful constructions with Legos. But, using the visual channel alone, he cannot learn sight words, nor can he learn sound-symbol correspondence.

---

[1] To clarify, in whole-language reading instruction, teachers read stories aloud to children, relying on repetition and recognition of words and phrases to embed themselves in students' minds. This differs from teaching children to "sound out" words (phonics).

Fortunately, we live in a time when such difficulties are under-stood and are no longer seen as indications of either stupidity or psychological block. Multisensory methods and materials, appro-priate—even vital—for learners like Benjy, are readily available and bring success. (See the material on multisensory learning for each grade level in part 2 of this book.)

Auditory Learning

The auditory system ferries sounds which the brain then regis-ters, interprets, and, sometimes, stores in memory. Accurate intake is vital for understanding. We need to remember that fre-quent middle-ear infections or allergies may distort or weaken the actual auditory signal.

As with the photocopier, some fortunate kids are born with a high-fidelity tape recorder. This machine has good volume con-trol, can record accurately, and can operate on fast-forward or replay. The tape is long enough to record what needs to be saved, and it captures sounds without crackle or fade out. There is ample cassette storage. These children hear something once and remember it.

Some bright kids have tape recorders that function poorly. Problems with volume or crackle may scramble incoming messages. (Janie tells me her favorite Christmas carol is "No Way in a Manger." This funny anecdote is a seri-ous matter because she makes this kind of error consistently.) Incorrect information liquefies the building blocks of con-ceptual foundations.

Other bright and available kids have a short tape, so they can only record small segments.

A Child "At Promise"

Lavinia, who could recite the alphabet at age two, is a walking songfest of nursery ditties and rhymes. She can follow and remember an age-appropriate explanation or set of directions, and as a kindergartner, could put her thoughts on paper in invented spelling because she heard the individual sounds in a word and could write them out in sequence. She learned to read easily using phonics (the study of spoken sounds). She is a rhythmic oral reader who naturally uses both cadence and inflection. Later on, she may do very well in the conversational aspects of foreign language. Although her auditory skills accompany good intelligence, they don't certify it. They are a convenience.

A Child "At Risk"

Mario drives his teacher to distraction with his frequent "What?" He and his third-grade classmates are expected to listen to explanations and then use the information. He maintains eye contact while the teacher is talking, but then says, "What are we supposed to do?" The shortness of his tape gets him in academic trouble and is unfairly earning him the inaccurate reputation of a kid who doesn't try.

Kinesthetic/Tactile Learning

Making contact with the physical world, the motor system gathers stimuli and learns patterns. The brain joins in to give them meaning and purpose. Fortunate kids have humming motors with oiled parts, precision gears, fully firing cylinders, and ample fuel.

These students harness their fine-motor skills to tasks of cutting, pasting, coloring, and, finally, writing. The Russian neurologist A. R. Luria described easy pencil control and hand-writing as "kinetic melody."

Some smart kids' motors run out of gas, or perhaps can putt-putt along on a straightaway, but they knock, shudder, or stall on a steep incline. This doesn't mean the children are stupid or lazy, in spite of the appearance of their written work. Being left-handed in a right-handed world compounds the problem, and—hard to believe but true—handwriting problems can come hand-in-hand (so to speak) with artistic skill in drawing, painting, sewing, or sculpting. Remember the 3-D/2-D discrepancy.

A Child "At Promise"

Sid's early childhood passion for vivid patterns in stringing wooden beads was a harbinger of skill with clay, paintbrushes, and felt tip markers in kindergarten, where he learned to write his three names (Sidney Elliott Halberstam) with grace, speed, and elegant spacing. In first grade, his creative writing was exceptional in both form and content, and he could guide his MicroMachines through intricate mazes he would build with his Lego set. His hand serves his brain beautifully, keeping pace with the developing rate and complexity of his ideas.

A Child "At Risk"

Jose's natural athletic ability has always helped him be a popular—even sought-after—member of the group. Now in fourth grade, he spends every free minute at the community center practicing basketball, soccer, or gymnastics. He is failing four subjects in school because his written work is so poor. He says, "If I'm just thinking about the shapes of the letters, I can write them. If I'm just thinking about how to spell one word, I can do it. If I'm just memorizing, I'm okay. If I'm just talking through some ideas,

I do well. But if I have to remember *and* think *and* spell *and* write, my fuses blow. My hand doesn't do what it's meant to, and I feel as if I have a hurricane in my head."

Multisensory training (described for each grade level in the second part of this book) would help him raise his mechanical skills to an automatic level, so all his attentional energy is free for thinking.

CHAPTER 5

EAGER TO MAKE CONNECTIONS

- filing
- retrieving
- recombining

What This Learning Pattern Is and Why It Matters

Children who make connections eagerly move from one subject to another—shifting from the vocabulary and concepts of math to those of language arts or social studies, adjusting their frames of reference when it's time to change classes. At the same time, they see how and why what they learned in social studies is useful in creative writing, or how the arithmetic they are learning in school parallels the way parents keep household accounts.

Eagerness to make connections is one of the hallmarks of intelligent thinking. It depends on being able to make distinctions, and on orderly filing, smooth retrieval, and ease in recombining.

Being disorganized is quicksand to efficient learning. Yet, many intelligent children have littered or misplaced mental files, thus their retrieval system—which may have been a grope-and-grab operation to begin with—is compromised. Not surprisingly, their efforts at recombining enjoy only irregular, sporadic success. These difficulties are exacerbated by (and often caused by) problems with language.

Filing

The efficient learner, who will make connections easily, mentally files emotional, physical, and intellectual experiences in an orderly way. Language is the foundation and the tool.

Categories for efficient filing include the six *wh* words (*who, what, when, where, why, how*). Who was involved—one or many? What was the main event? When did it occur? Where did it take place? Why does it matter? How does it relate to other experiences or perceptions?

Retrieving

Smooth memory function allows a thinker to fish out needed information from the vast mental pool of personal experience, emotion, and thought. And, of course, effortless retrieval depends on orderly filing. Otherwise, retrieval is like rummaging around in the socks drawer at night with no lights on.

For students, disruptions of retrieval can be embarrassing, annoying, or disastrous.

Some people have trouble with rote memory. Even though they have wide and accurate memory for experiences and feelings, they have trouble memorizing arithmetic combinations, lists of presidents or monarchs in succession, or scientific formulae.

Others may have trouble with target-word retrieval. They know exactly what they want to say, but the necessary word is "just on the tip of their tongue." Memory and retrieval may be persistently elusive or be prompted by a tiny hint.

Eddie was trying to tell his class that his family needed the plumber to come quickly to fix a leak in the valve of the dishwasher. He said, "He came, you know . . . he had to, we had to . . . you know, get him there in a hurry, the man who . . . who . . . you know, who, um, fixes those things." (His listeners were totally confused.) "And, he used a, a thing (*demonstrating*), and my mom was so glad it was, well, no more water on the floor."

His teacher said, "It sounds as if you needed a special fixer. Let's see if we can help you remember what that kind of fixer is called. Is he an electrician or a pl—?"

"Yes! Yes! It's a plumber! We had to get the plumber fast."

Recombining

Originality and creativity are expressed through the formation of novel combinations of ideas, concepts, or experiences. The thinker/learner files, retrieves, and then recombines. Doing this with efficiency, as well as enthusiasm, requires systematic filing to begin with, then precision in retrieval, and finally the new and personal idea.

Neurologists are now exploring the concept of convergent zones—interconnections of thought that give many dimensions to a single word or object. For example, the word *cup* may call to mind the function of a cup, or the physical properties of a cup, or the type of cup the listener or reader owns or aspires to own, or the shape of the word in print, or the string of sounds necessary to speak or spell *cup,* or words which rhyme with *cup.* The list is endless. Of course, the greater the number of associations, the richer the web of convergent zones, and the greater the variety and texture of thought available to the thinker.

A Child "At Promise"

Shoshana is a delight to her teacher, a savior to her friends, and a pleasure to herself. Generous with her creative output, she makes novel combinations with ease; she remembers facts, concepts, and ideas from numerous sources; and she files them in memory quickly and accurately.

Although her desk is not necessarily the tidiest in fourth grade, she remembers the page numbers of the homework assignment; she knows how many days remain until the class trip; she can locate the states on a map; she knows the product of 7 x 8; she can recite large chunks of Dr. Seuss; for a book report, she wrote a limerick apiece about each of the major characters in *The Wind in the Willows.*

A Child "At Risk"

Todd has had a wide variety of experiences in his eight years. He has flown to Disney World, learned to ski in Vermont, spent a week on a working farm, visited his grandparents who live in Washington, D.C., and seen the Capitol's tourist sights in an age-appropriate way. He owns a junior atlas and a junior encyclopedia, and enjoys browsing through both. He watches TV and also hit the top rung of the ladder at the neighborhood library's Climb with Stories. Intelligent, available, and original, he nonetheless is driving his parents and teachers up the wall.

In discussion, he jumps from idea to idea—not the purposeful shortcut of linear leapfrogging—but more like a grasshopper. He jumps, and it's hard to know where he'll land. He has an enormous store of general information, which he often has trouble cataloging and retrieving. His rote memory for facts is very poor, yet he drew from memory one of Leonardo's designs for a flying machine.

When he is excited, his ideas tumble in a torrent; he has trouble getting them down on paper rapidly enough to catch them all. At such times, his handwriting gets messy, his spelling becomes truncated, and his ideas are disorganized. He receives very poor grades.

Complex problems resist simplistic solutions, but in part 2— "Addressing Learning Patterns, Meeting Needs, and Having Fun"—you will find practical tips that will help your child if her experience is similar to Todd's.

CHAPTER 6

GIFTED, PRECOCIOUS, OR JUST PLAIN SMART

What This Learning Pattern Is and Why It Matters

Mercifully, we are rid of the limiting notion that highly intelligent people wear horn-rimmed glasses, live in the library, have pasty complexions, spout facts from memory, and get perfect scores on tests. Wider, deeper, broader perceptions are our gifts from several notable researchers, among them Howard Gardner, codirector of Project Zero at Harvard.

Gardner is the author of many books, including *Frames of Mind: The Theory of Multiple Intelligences* and *The Unschooled Mind: How Children Think and How Schools Should Teach.*

In *Frames of Mind,* Gardner asserts that humans possess at least seven separate intelligences, only two of which influence grade-point averages or are factored into the formula for being on the honor roll. The intelligences are:

- logical/mathematical
- linguistic
- musical

- spatial
- bodily/kinesthetic
- interpersonal
- intrapersonal

The positive aspects of the traits may be camouflaged. Teachers may be impatient with the different learning rhythms and avenues of thinking these children express. Of course, we can see that from the five nonacademic intelligences come some of society's most valued insights and inventions.

In harmony with Gardner, and moving far beyond restricting intelligence to a single numerical score, Joseph Renzulli at the University of Connecticut offers his three-circle model, interconnecting above-average intelligence, task commitment, and creativity.

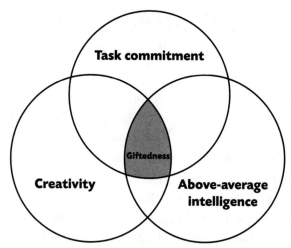

He suggests that giftedness is released where all three interconnect.

In years of studying and working with the education of the gifted, I have collected ten traits, clusters of which appear in gifted thinkers of all ages. Not necessarily convenient, and sometimes annoying all the way round in spite of being exhilarating, the ten are:

- rapid grasp of concepts
- awareness of patterns
- drive
- concentration
- energy
- curiosity
- empathy
- vulnerability
- heightened perceptions
- divergent thinking

Fortunate the child whose talents and interests match family and community priorities, as well as the intellectual/academic opportunities at school. Children whose minds work more quickly than their peers' have a low tolerance for pedantry, boredom, and repetition. While repetition is a necessary part of teaching and learning for many students, for these it is an irritation sufficient enough to turn them away from the task at hand. Additionally, children who are naturally drawn to concepts or activities not valued by their school or family feel discomfort, which often blooms into mistrust—of themselves or of the institutions which would otherwise support them. That's why we need to examine these patterns here.

A word of caution. Some children, more often girls than boys, are verbally precocious. This skill in delivery and size of vocabulary may create the impression of high overall intelligence or giftedness. But a major identifying hallmark of giftedness is the ability to use and enjoy concepts, not simply to recite facts. In fairness to small spouters, we must probe for their enjoyment of thinking, even as we marvel at their conversation.

A Child "At Promise"

From his earliest years, Scott was interested in numbers. He counted early, was quick to see number patterns, could ramble forward or backward on his mental number line, and intuitively knew how to multiply and divide as well as add or subtract.

Scott's father is an engineer, his mother teaches music. Family conversation and activities matched Scott's natural interests. In school, he used manipulative materials (blocks, dice, inch cubes, and poker chips) for true mathematical exploration, and was allowed to progress through the math lab materials at his own pace once his daily work was done. Needless to say, he is flourishing, and his teachers are helping him move laterally to widen his conceptual base, rather than taking the more obvious path of vertical acceleration.

A Child "At Risk"

Catherine has always loved costumes, stories, playacting, and dancing. When she was four, she had what she called her "twirling skirt." She would spin around and delight in seeing the material flare out from her body. She would be a parasol, a Ferris wheel, a whirlpool, a merry-go-round, a fairy princess, or in one instance, both Sleeping Beauty and the spinning wheel. She would dance out stories either from books or from her head. When she outgrew the skirt, she kept it in her costume box and would wear it on her head or on an arm. To her, it was a prop of limitless scope.

Her school, like many today, is overcrowded. Children sit at desks in rows and read aloud when called on. Each child is responsible for large amounts of "seat work": ditto sheets, workbook pages, phonics exercises—but very few stories. Her teacher is a rigid person with too many students. She maintains order by imposing silence and strict rules.

Both of Catherine's parents work and feel compelled to use Saturdays for catching up on errands. On most Sundays, they go to church, then visit a nearby grandparent, then go to the park where Catherine's two older brothers can run off steam. Her parents say, "It's time for her to grow out of all that babyish pretending."

Pretending is valuable. In addition to being fun, it forms a channel through which creative imagination flows, irrigating the soil of reading comprehension and writing competence, and opening up wide fields of knowledge. From history to literature to political science, joyful understanding depends on being able to identify with characters, situations, places, or times—pretending.

Abilities that are undervalued or repressed shrivel and die, or turn rancid as they are denied sun and air. Catherine's lovely talent is in serious jeopardy.

PART 2

ADDRESSING LEARNING PATTERNS, MEETING NEEDS, AND HAVING FUN

So what's a parent to do? This section is about learning patterns without tears. Here come the promised, tested, and trenches-validated 142 practical tips and activities.

These tips and activities will help you:

- learn more about your child's learning patterns;
- provide opportunities to build your child's natural strengths and bolster weaknesses;
- liberate your child's learning patterns for optimal learning—both at home and at school.

If you find any activities that your child really enjoys (2-D activities, for example), share the information with your child's teachers. They will benefit from the insight you've discovered about your child's learning pattern, and they might be willing to incorporate similar activities into the classroom routine.

First, we will consider twenty-two General Principles of Good Practice, which apply across the grades. Because each is important, I have purposely not tried to rank them hierarchically.

Then, moving grade by grade from kindergarten through fourth grade, I will lay out the major focus of each year's curriculum, making at least three suggestions apiece for each of the six learning patterns previously discussed. Thus, for example, I will describe the probable emphasis of third grade, then make three suggestions for fostering availability, three strategies for bridging the 3-D/2-D gap, three for simultaneous and sequential processing, and so forth. The idea is to speculate, investigate, and generate, and when the suggestions for each grade level are combined with the principles of good practice, a grand total of 142 practical tips and activities is the result.

The curriculum sequence outlined here follows general common practice. If this moves faster than your child's school does, don't be concerned; simply look at the suggestions for earlier levels. If your child's school is ahead, flip forward. There is nothing sacred about specific content at specific levels. There is everything sacred about building foundations of competence in an orderly way.

CHAPTER 7

GENERAL PRINCIPLES OF GOOD PRACTICE

1. Play with taking words apart and putting them back together. For example, if your child is in kindergarten or first grade, you might say, "I'll say a word. You tell me how many syllables it has. Ready? *Pic-nic.* Good. You're right, it has two syllables." If your child is in second or third grade, you might say, "I'm going to say a word. Please count the syllables, and then I'm going to ask you to say back one of those syllables to me. Ready? *Thanksgiving.* Yes, three is right. Please say the second one. Right, *giv* is the second syllable." When your child is in fourth grade he will be able to count the syllables, select out one, and then spell it. For example, "*Television,* count the syllables, and spell the final one. Good, four syllables in all, and the final one is spelled *s-i-o-n.*"

2. Read aloud. No child is too old to hear the beauty and power of language. This is superb preparation for later independent reading and should be a regular part of your home routine. This is an area where you can really help. But if family realities make this unrealistic, I encourage you to get your child good audiotapes. When you and your child listen to a story together—at home or on car trips—it's amazing how many fights don't happen.

3. Create a climate in which your child is willing to take risks. Remember the power of the limbic system, the emotional brain.

4. Take advantage of exercises that honor originality over conformity. If everyone's doing the same thing and shooting for the same goal, competition becomes dominant. Open-ended questions, creative writing, and inventing mythical new products are but a few of the avenues to originality that you can use to entice your child.

5. Create showcases for your child's talent. Try to find ways to weave your child's strengths into the fabric of daily living.

6. Let your child make some of the decisions. *Learning* is an active verb. Education isn't something to be painted on from the outside.

7. Use visual aids to help reinforce what your child is learning in school. For example, find pictures of the areas she is studying in social studies. Hang a big calendar and refer to it frequently. Use the globe and maps as well as spoken and written words. Your local library may also have reproductions of famous works of art you can borrow.

8. Measures of mastery should be wide and rich, giving your child a chance to enjoy showing what he's learned. Let him demonstrate—through exhibitions, portfolios, and

other products of his hands—how he has grown in his mind and imagination. Let him be the curator of the refrigerator-door museum.

9. Provide opportunities for 3-D hands-on learning. (See suggestions for each grade in the following chapters.)

10. Use math manipulatives (buttons, poker chips, inch cubes, dice, and playing cards) all the way through. They show and tell the intricacies of counting, adding, subtracting, seeing patterns, and combining the intellectual energies of math with just plain fun.

11. When you are helping your child with a homework assignment, discuss the purpose of the lesson before she starts. Delineate the whole concept as well as the little increments—provide both an umbrella and a road map. You can do this with home activities and games, as well.

12. Allow for humor. Not only is it a face saver, it's a dowser's wand to the pools of affect and energy that characterize real learning.

13. Help your child memorize poetry, and provide opportunities for recitation. A child who knows something "by heart" has a permanent gift and resource to use for pure pleasure, for passing boring time in a traffic jam, or, as an adult, for distraction in such situations as timing labor pains.

14. Stress connections among various disciplines. Too often, we hear children say, "Oh, yeah, but I only do that in math class." If you want learning to stick—to become part of your child's personal, fundamental matrix—you must show him how ideas and knowledge cut across lines and interconnect.

15. Show your child how to visualize while listening—to exercise the mind's eye.

16. Teach your child these four steps to better listening skills:
1) Make a mental movie.
2) Repeat back to yourself what you have heard.
3) Make a rebus or small drawing (introduction to note taking).
4) Ask for a repetition.

17. Take some chances yourself. Try some new ideas. Trust in your child. Keep alive the creativity and compassion in your life. Don't let it suffocate.

18. Be sure your child understands your family's philosophical priorities on education and your practical requirements on such issues as TV, amount of sleep, homework. Be sure you know them yourself.

19. Think hard about the difference between the parent as coach and the parent as captor. Which role enhances learning?

20. Help your child organize herself in time and space. She needs to know when things will happen, how much time is needed for various tasks, where to keep her belongings, where to put her homework when it has been completed, where to keep any ongoing projects. The late Harriet Sheridan, a dean from Brown University, urged early and constant training in temporal and spatial organization. She said it is helpful in elementary school, convenient in middle school, supportive in high school, and *vital* for college success. That being the case, the earlier you begin (in an age-appropriate way), the more you help your child.

21. Teach your child the *how*'s instead of the *what*'s. *How*'s confer power on the learner.

22. Enjoy the messiness of questions as well as the tidiness of answers.

CHAPTER 8

KINDERGARTEN

Curriculum Overview

The kindergarten curriculum generally focuses on the social skills necessary for group participation, on the listening and speaking aspects of language development, on counting, and on reading readiness skills. Some kindergartens have formal reading programs; others allow room for ready children to read but don't expect everyone to do so.

Kindergarten children need a strong language base, and those whose language—either receptive or expressive—is weak may scrape along at this early level, but will stumble later. Vigilant attention to your kindergarten child's language levels pays off now and later.

Practical Suggestions for Six Learning Patterns

Available for Schoolwork

■ physically

- emotionally
- intellectually

1. Check out your child's hearing, vision, sleep, diet. Provide simple snacks for your child to bring to school.

2. Nothing succeeds like success. Get a large piece of brown paper and ask your child to lie down on it while another family member traces the outline of his body. Fill in what he is wearing, his hair and eye color, etc. Then each member of the family tells why this person is special. The parents write their ideas. Hang the portrait cum comments on the refrigerator door for a week.

3. Honor each family member's ideas. This implies establishing clear rules about listening to one another.

Three-Dimensional or Two-Dimensional

1. Join the symbols your child is learning to his own experience and knowledge. For example, help your child learn the sounds of the letters by using a material whose name starts with the sound the letter makes: paste cotton balls in the shape of a *c* on a card to teach the sound of *c*, paste stick-on dots in the shape of a *d* on a card to teach the sound of *d*, glue a piece of string on a card in the shape of an *s* to teach that sound. (A complete list of clues can be found in my book *Common Ground*.) Keep the clue cards together on a notebook ring.

2. Check out your child's understanding of the language of time and space. Can she make sentences or phrases using *today, tomorrow, yesterday, morning, afternoon, noon, last night, after lunch, before snack, until the music stops*? This is the time to solidify your child's knowledge of the days of the week, using a calendar large enough for your child to see easily.

Can she make phrases or sentences using *here, there, where, big, bigger, biggest, these, those, over, under, around, inside, outside, on top of,* etc.?

In many ways, English is a tricky language. We use the words of space to refer to time: *around two o'clock, on the dot,* and even *on time!*

3. Provide many opportunities for your child to hear stories and then act them out. As we saw in Catherine's story on pages 44 and 45, pretending is a noble activity.

Simultaneous or Sequential

1. Be sure your child knows what words do and are, and how and why letters go together to construct words. Don't take this understanding for granted. Ask "What is a word?" "What is reading?" One five-year-old said, "Reading is something on paper that you do. Words are what you say to people." Asked whether they were connected, she said, "No. Talking is out loud, and when you read, people are supposed to be quiet."

2. Practice stringing sounds together with your child to make serious or silly words (*l-e-g, h-a-t, g-l-o-b, d-e-s-k, s-p-l-u-n-k*), and practice breaking words into chunks (*picnic/pic-nic, trumpet/trum-pet, cucumber/cu-cum-ber*). Your child might struggle over this seemingly simple task. Don't force the issue, but start to train him.

3. Your kindergartner needs plenty of time for arts and crafts and plenty of time to play with blocks and Legos. Don't be surprised if you hear her saying, "Flowers and stars," as she paints, and, "Hey, here come the bad guys. This is the jail. Wait. I'll put extra doors so they can't get out. Here's the ramp. Here comes the car. Watch out!" Connections among language, hands-on experience, and imagination are intellectual, emotional, and linguistic nourishment to the young child.

Multisensory

- visual
- auditory
- kinesthetic/tactile

Visual

1. Use yellow Post-it notes to label objects around the house (or your child's bedroom or play space). The young child with a crisp mental photocopying machine will learn and retain the images of the words *desk, table, toy box, bookshelf, globe,* etc.

2. Use picture naming books, such as those by Richard Scarry.

3. Go on pattern hunts with your child: "Let's see how many things we can find that are the shape of a circle, a triangle, a square."

Auditory

1. Play I Packed My Grandmother's Trunk. You and your child can play this game together, or gather other family members to play as well. In this old-fashioned, perennially amusing game, player one starts, "I packed my grandmother's trunk, and in it I put . . . (perhaps) an albatross." Player two repeats the refrain, and continuing the pattern, adds a contribution: "I packed my grandmother's trunk and in it I put an albatross and a banana." The next player must remember and recite, "I packed my grandmother's trunk and in it I put an albatross, a banana, and a coconut." The suggestions needn't follow alphabetical order; in fact, it's better if they don't at this age. The object of the game is to be able to hear, remember, and recite the items others have packed in that trunk. (Speaking as a grandmother, I hope they don't pack for me!) The game is over when a player repeats an item already mentioned or cannot recall the items recited.

2. Read and sing stories with refrains or other opportunities for "audience participation." Songs that incorporate counting give listener-singers a structure for support. For example, your kindergartner probably loves, "This old man, he played one, he played knick-knack on my thumb . . ."

3. Help your child play with the locations of sounds within familiar words. Use small blocks or tiles in five colors to help him see both the location and sequence of the sounds he hears.

When your child practices counting the number of sounds in a word, and noticing where those sounds sit in the sequence which forms that word, he is expanding his ability to read and to write. Auditory analysis is the foundation of much reading, writing, and spelling.

Start with a three-letter word and three blocks in three different colors (the different colors represent the different sounds). Say, "I'm going to show you how to build the word *cat.*

I'll put a green block first for the /c/ sound, I'll add a yellow block for the /a/ sound, and I'll put a red block at the end for the /t/ sound. I can spread my blocks apart in a long line or push them together in one unit. They'll still represent the same word."

Then say to your child, "Which block would I have to change if I want to turn *cat* into *bat?* Yes, the first one, and I couldn't use either yellow or red, could I? Those already represent sounds. So go ahead, change *cat* into *bat.* Now which block would you have to switch if you wanted to change *bat* into *bag?* Good. Do it. Now which block would you have to move to change *bag* into *beg?* Can you change *beg* into *begs?*"

Start with *and,* then add blocks to create the new word. Change *and* into *land,* change *land* into *sand,* change *sand* into *stand,* change *stand* into *stands.* Yes, the first and last blocks must be the same color.

Kinesthetic/Tactile

1. Teach sound/symbol correspondence and letter formation by using the large muscles of the arm to "skywrite." The letters formed in the air should be as large as the arc of your child's swing. Teach a little verbal accompaniment such as "*d* starts the way *c* starts, closes the circle, goes all the way up to the top line, and back down."

2. Beware of splinter skills, little shards of the major skill you want your child to develop. Splinter skills emerge when your child is moved too quickly from the large-motor work of skywriting or jumbo blackboard writing, to small-letter formation with adult-sized pencils on paper with small spaces between lines. Early splinter skills lead to subsequent cramped and uncomfortable handwriting.

3. If your child is not a natural athlete, be alert to the possibility that she might face some awkward social situations at school. Children who are not physically coordinated often must make public display of what they do poorly in front of the people they're trying to make friends with. You must find other strengths in your child and find a way to showcase those abilities.

Eager to Make Connections

1. Play as many games as possible that involve categories. You might say, "Let's try I Packed My Grandmother's Trunk, and only put in things to eat, or things to wear, or barnyard animals."

2. Play Collector. Say to your child, "I'm going to say a category. You think of as many words as possible to add to our collection that fit my category. I'll give you hints if you get stuck. Ready? My category is 'things you find in the kitchen.'" Your child might produce a word collection for this category that includes: cereal, spoons, knives, bowls, glasses, plates, toaster ovens, microwave ovens, stoves, refrigerators, dishwashers, wastebaskets, recycling bins, salt, dishtowels, clocks, telephones, and cookbooks.

3. Have or make a puppet theater. It can be as simple as a desk or table. The desktop is the stage floor, your child sits on the floor behind the desk, and the puppet(s) prance as the director—your child—wishes.

Gifted, Precocious, or Just Plain Smart

- factual
- aesthetic
- imaginary

1. Keep a piece of paper titled "Proclivities Profile" for your child. List three talents or interests she shows. Periodically add to the list (perhaps two or three times a year). Keep the tally going throughout your child's academic career. See which patterns remain and which shift.

2. Help your child participate in arenas he might not be drawn to on his own. Declare a baking afternoon or a lawn maintenance afternoon one Saturday.

3. Exercise divergent thinking through Recycling Art. Keep a big plastic garbage bag to store cardboard toilet paper rolls, old unmatched earrings, bits of yarn, and so forth. Ask your child to create a space shuttle, a new world, a habitation for an animal, whatever tickles your—and her—fancy. Take Polaroid pictures of your child's final product and post it on the refrigerator or some other public domain where your child can receive praise for her work.

CHAPTER 9

FIRST GRADE

Curriculum Overview

In first grade, the focus of the curriculum is integrating pre-reading skills into the combined processes of reading, writing, spelling, and pencil-paper arithmetic. Therefore, multisensory materials are appropriate or even ideal for all children in the regular classroom. Even though these materials were originally designed for a special population, any group they serve well is special itself because of its special success. Top first graders, middle group children, slower students . . . the robins, the eagles, the bluejays—all benefit.

The use of individual contracts promotes feelings of autonomy, and the principles of cooperative learning foster group problem-solving skills. In first grade, teachers will focus on fortifying their students' language development and building group identity, often by reading aloud *to* the children. Emphasis is also placed on liberating imagination through creative writing, as well as reinforcing the links among emotion, printed words, and physical experience. Just as first graders are ready to develop (and need to practice) respect for self and others, their teachers need to expect and tolerate different rates of learning and levels of competence.

Children soar when teachers combine training in the mechanical skills with excursions into imagination.

Practical Suggestions for Six Learning Patterns

Available for Schoolwork

- physically
- emotionally
- intellectually

1. During a visit to your child's school, ask where he sits, and check the height of his desk and chair to make sure there's a good match between his body size and the furniture. Check the position of your child's seat in the room. Can he see the board? If your child has a history of recurrent ear infections or documented hearing problems, ask your child's teacher if he can sit in the front of the room, so he can make eye contact and not be distracted by peripheral noise.

2. Acknowledge the power and universality of negative as well as positive emotions. When you legitimize turbulent feelings by exploring them in literature, your child will find it easier to accept herself and others. Folktales and fairy tales are ideal.

3. Offer your child open-ended opportunities, rather than loading him up with canned questions demanding single correct answers. Start with, "What would happen if . . ." Add, "It stayed light all day and never ever got dark?" or "Your first three wishes of every day would come true." Or "You received a personal and secret invitation to go through a time warp?"

You can provide the situation three or four times, then ask your child for his suggestions on how to complete the question/phrase. One idea per week carbonates family conversation.

Your child can give his ideas and answers in spoken or written words, pictures, songs, commercials, etc.

Three-Dimensional or Two-Dimensional

1. Ask your child to make a map of her bedroom. Show her how architects mark windows and doors. Have your child put her bed, dresser, desk, bookcases, and other bedroom furniture in place. Then ask her to put a circle in her favorite color on the place she spends the most time. Have your child choose the wall she likes the best and then draw that in elevation (how she sees it face-on, as opposed to the floor plan she has just done). Ask her to use colored markers or pens to add in three things she thinks would be improvements.

2. Make charts of color and number words for your child. For colors, on the left-hand side of the chart write the names of the colors, using a pen of the same color. On the right-hand side, color in a square of the color.

   For numbers, on the left-hand side of the chart write the number word, in the middle draw that number of buttons or sticks, and on the right-hand side draw the configuration of the number as it appears on dice. For example:

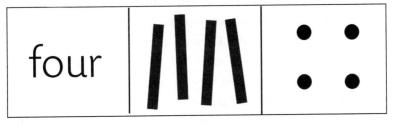

3. To distinguish left from right, let your child put a (loose) Red Rubber band on his Right wRist. If you are concerned that the rubber band may impede circulation, have your child use a Red Ribbon instead.

Simultaneous or Sequential

1. Together with your child, start a simple weather station. Each day, help your child measure and record the temperature, the precipitation, and the overall climate. Have him chart the results on a wall calendar, color coding each type of information. Every week or so, review the weather history and—tying the discussion to the rotating seasons of the year—ask your child to make some predictions. Check on his accuracy later.

2. Make a board game of your child's routine weekend activities. Include the words and a corresponding rebus, or picture, for each activity. For example, your child's routine might include the following: wake-up time, homework time, visiting with friends, athletics, chore time, feeding the pet, straightening up her room, bedtime. Using an open manila folder, draw the game path moving from upper left to lower right, sprinkle the activities along the path in random order, and throw in a few hazards such as "Bad cold. Stay in bed all day. Miss one turn."

Then play the game with your child. Initially, you and your child should simply go around the board, reading the descriptions of the spots you land on. When your child can do that, up the ante. For example, say, "Today you have to say what comes just before the activity you land on. If you land on bedtime, you have to remember what you do just before bedtime, and name that activity." Then use *after.* Or require your child to say one positive and one negative comment about that activity. The only limit here is your imagination.

3. Every once in a while, post the instructions for a craft project. One chart should be in pictures, the other in words. Have the materials handy. See if your child can complete the project using the pictorial or verbal instructions without help from you. For example, Make a Yarn Octopus.

Verbal Instructions

1. Take yarn and wind a twelve-inch loop.
2. Do this continuously at least thirty-two times.
3. Mark off the top third.
4. Tie tightly with another piece of yarn. Leave a bow.
5. Cut the bottom of the lower loops.
6. Separate loose strands into eight equal bundles.
7. Tie each bundle.
8. Add eyes.

Pictorial Instructions

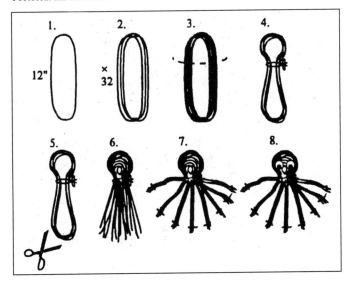

Multisensory

- visual
- auditory
- kinesthetic/tactile

Visual

1. Using index cards, write sight words (words that we recognize without stopping to sound them out) in pairs for your child to practice while playing Concentration. Select sight words for your cards from the Dolch Sight Word list in appendix B. See activity 3 on page 85 for Concentration instructions.

2. Ask your child to observe as many details as possible about your appearance, clothing, hairstyle, etc. Leave the room and either switch or remove something, then come back into the room and ask your child to see if she can spot what's different.

3. To help your child learn sight words, use a Bingo format and follow this progression: *match, select, read, spell.*

Make a nine-space Bingo card. Put your child's name in the middle and select eight words to teach. (See the Dolch Sight Word list in appendix B for suggestions.) Write one word in each of the spaces. Cut index cards into nine slips the same size as the Bingo spaces. Help your child copy each word onto one of the slips. Then turn the slips face down on the table or desk. Ask your child to pick a slip, turn it word side up, and match the slip to the space with the same word.

When your child can do that, give him nine tokens. You call a word, he selects the word you have said, putting a token on that space.

Next, you put a token on a space, and your child must read the word.

Finally, you cover a space and say the word, and your child must spell it.

Your child might whiz through the progression and learn a year's worth of sight words effortlessly. Or your child might need to move much more slowly. Games are excellent learning tools as long as they are fun. When fear comes in, joy goes out. Don't rush!

Auditory

1. Open a manila file folder lengthwise. On it, in descending order, write the daily order of your child's home activities, with a corresponding rebus for each. At the start of the day, open the folder and say, "Here's a picture of what you're going to be doing today." Pointing at each with your finger, go down the list. When you come to an activity that happens only on certain days (such as sports practice or music lessons), skip it.

   Why does this help? First, it gives your child a picture/map of what she will be doing. Second, if your child has trouble remembering the sequence of the day, she can check for herself. Third, if she is straying from the proper task, you have only to point to the picture of the current activity and make a silence sign. Fourth, if reading is hard and snack time is heaven, your child can easily see how soon relief is coming.

Here's what a sample activity list looks like:

Wake up

Eat breakfast

LIBERATE YOUR CHILD'S LEARNING PATTERNS

Go to school

Have an after-school snack

Play outside

Do homework

Eat dinner

Talk to friends

Take a shower or bath

Listen to tapes or watch television

Bedtime

2. Play Mad Libs. In this suspenseful language game, you read a story in which you substitute blanks for such key words as adjectives, nouns, and verbs. When you reach a blank, elicit words in the appropriate category from your child, and at the end, read him his completed story.

Substitute the phrases "a describing word" or "an action word" for such terms as adjectives and adverbs. Before reading the filled-in version, find out how accurate your child can be in remembering his contributions: "Tommy, can you remember the proper noun you chose?" Then read the product. Laughter, recognition, and a bit of suspense are key ingredients in a recipe for enthusiastic listening.

3. Play I'm Thinking of a Number. Think of a number between 1 and 100. See how quickly your child can identify it. Teach her strategies for narrowing the field by asking big-yield questions such as, "Is it after 50?" That eliminates one half of the choices in one fell swoop. "Is it an even number?" There goes another 50 percent. Let's say your child has established that the number is odd and below 50; show her how to reduce by half again. "Is it 25 or below?" If she asks, "Is it 77?" you can reply, "Is 77 below 50?" and reinforce the value of listening and trying to keep the clues in mind. (It helps some kids to visualize a number line and record the clues on it.) Next, show your child how to establish which decade the number is in. "Is it a single number?" If the answer is negative, there is a maximum of eight choices (11, 13, 15, 17, 19, 21, 23, 25). "Is it a teen?" If not, only three possibilities remain. "Is it 23 or lower?" If your answer is no again, the number has to be 25.

Too complicated for a first grader? No. Particularly if she has a number line available and is encouraged to use her fingers.

Then have your child think of the next number and answer the questions while you try to guess the number.

Kinesthetic/Tactile

1. Play Snap, Snap, Clap, Clap. In this adaptation of an old drinking song, you establish a category and then ask your child to join in with the refrain and be ready in turn to name an object belonging to the designated category.

For example, you might say, "My category is food. Think of three or four possibilities in case I use your idea. Now snap your fingers twice and clap your hands twice in rhythm and name a food." After snapping and clapping, your child might say, "bananas." In return, after snapping and clapping, you might say, "pickles." Next, she might respond "chips," and so forth. When one of you repeats a word that has already been said, the game is over.

2. Your child should learn to put a green dot (go) on the upper left-hand corner of worksheets and assignments. This shows him where to start, and therefore which direction to go. If your child is right-handed, show him how to slant the paper so the lower left-hand corner faces his belt buckle. If your child is left-handed, he should slant the paper so the lower right-hand corner lines up with his belt buckle. This prevents the development of a hook.

You should reinforce correct pencil grip. If an incorrect one is deeply ingrained, it's probably too late to effect a change, but it's worth a try. Remember, your influence is extensive. A chat can save hours of attempted reconstruction.

3. Clump and practice letters of similar size or line orientation. "Let's collect a list of all the tall letters (*b, d, f, g, k, l, t*)." Or, "Today we'll work on letters that drop below the line (*g, j, p, q, y*)." Or, "This is small-letter day (*a, c, e, i, m, n, o, r, s, u, v, w, x, z*)."

Eager to Make Connections

- filing
- retrieving
- recombining

1. Your first-grade child will profit from practice in following directions. Here's an exercise that joins imagination and obedience.

Have your child start with a blank piece of unlined 8½" x 11" paper. Following is a typical set of directions:

Fold the paper in half lengthwise and make a crease; fold it again bottom to top and make another crease. Open the paper out and put it flat on the table. Using a red crayon, number the sections 1, 2, 3, 4. In section 1, draw three things you would play with outside. In section 2, write the name of a friend and draw something that person would like to get as a birthday present. In section 3, write the even numbers between 20 and 30, write what you would get if you added 3 and 4, and draw a circle around that answer. In section 4, draw a picture of yourself in your favorite clothes.

2. Pick an adjective and ask your child to think of as many objects as possible that fit the description. For example, starting with *slimy*, your child might produce: *worms, spaghetti, frogs, soap that's been left in the bathtub, the insides of pumpkins, seaweed, bugs, live fish, raw chicken, those liquid cherries inside chocolate candies, asparagus, dog drool, pond scum.*

Write each one on an index card and put the index cards in a paper bag. Have your child pick a card, read it silently, and then write five descriptive sentences to fit that object. Have her read the Collections of Five aloud, and then you try to figure out which slimy object she selected.

For example, if your child picked "live fish," her sentences might be:

It feels cold and clammy.
It tastes good when my dad cooks it on the grill.
Cleaning it is GROSS!
It has eyeballs.
It lives in cold mud in the winter.

3. Have your child pick one of the five sentences from the previous activity to use as a title to describe something else. For example, say your child chooses "It has eyeballs." She might write, "It has eyeballs. Two of them. When it cries, tears come out of its eyeballs. This creature's eyes are blue, they follow me around the room when the creature sits in his high chair. The creature is my baby brother."

Gifted, Precocious, or Just Plain Smart

- factual
- aesthetic
- imaginary

1. Give your first grader a chance to do independent, individual work. Have him choose an animal to be the subject of a report. The report can be as simple or as complicated as your child prefers. Have your child present his work to you or a group of family members.

2. Read a story aloud without showing the pictures to your child. Next, read the story again, and have her pantomime all the characters, actions, and scenes. Then ask your child

to choose at least one character or element from the story to illustrate or describe in writing. Incorporate your child's illustration(s) or description(s) into another reading of the story.

3. Give your child a paper bag filled with six or seven surprise props, such as a fireman's hat, some high-heeled shoes, a baby blanket, an eggbeater, a camera, a book, and a clock. Your child's job is to invent a story that will make use of the entire collection and either tell it to you and other interested family members, holding up the props as necessary, or—much more fun—costume herself in the props and turn the story into a play, which she acts out.

CHAPTER 10

SECOND GRADE

Curriculum Overview

In second grade, the focus of the curriculum is integrating early reading skills and bringing them to an automatic level. Young readers polish the rhythm, cadence, and expression of their oral reading, and the accuracy and comfort of their silent reading. When the teacher reads aloud to the class, the students will enjoy exercising their minds' eyes and also anticipating what's to come. Collectively, a shiver of delicious fear will ripple through them as the giant's footsteps grow louder, or as the leak in the boat gets bigger and bigger.

Multisensory methods and materials continue to be appropriate for teaching the mechanical aspects of language arts: decoding (reading), encoding (spelling and speaking), and writing. During second grade, many children begin to reach "kinetic melody" as their handwriting becomes evenly shaped, easily legible, and comfortable to produce. That is, of course, if schools play fair.

In the past, many schools have taught manuscript (or printing) in kindergarten, first, and early second grade. Then, usually around February, the teacher says, "Have I got a surprise for you! Now I'm going to teach you cursive (or script)." She teaches the letter formation, but the students are expected to keep on using manuscript. Thus, they are learning something but not using it, and their handwriting practice or instruction time is spent on something different from what they are expected to produce.

This is a hangover from the era of needing to know manuscript for making scientific labels and needing cursive as a badge of culture and education. We have continued dragging this dinosaur carcass through our second- and third-grade classrooms, and the children find it increasingly cumbersome. They end up unsure of both written systems, comfortable with neither, and only semiskilled in an area that should be double-strength. Do you know the policy on teaching handwriting at your child's school?

Enlightened policy suggests each school should choose one handwriting system (we could argue the merits for each endlessly), teach it, give students opportunities to practice and polish it until it is automatic, then teach keyboard fingering, and finally teach word processing. When children with weak or marginal handwriting turn away from pencil and paper to the computer, they invariably develop their own system of hunt and peck, which is nearly impossible to eradicate and which leaves them hobbled in their area of greatest need. Second grade is the time to prevent unnecessary trouble and to continue to bring a necessary skill to a comfortable level.

Second graders, prone to moodiness themselves, like predictability and routine. They like to know what's expected, where the limits are, and the consequences of transgression. They find structure supportive, not repressive.

Wise teachers will accommodate a rather wide range of competencies and look beneath the surface in predicting future accomplishment. Some children—particularly little boys—with the capacity to become strong students in later years may still struggle with some of the mechanics. Other students may be mechanically adept but intellectually timid.

Practical Suggestions for Six Learning Patterns

Available for Schoolwork

- physically
- emotionally
- intellectually

1. If your child has allergies, it is important to find out if there is a pet animal in the classroom. Air dandered by Snuffles the guinea pig—or scented by his cedar shavings—may be enough to throw your child seriously off track.

2. Children find solace in the company of friends. Don't we all? Ask your child to draw a picture of a favorite stuffed animal. Make a stack of photocopies from the drawing that your child can color or leave in black and white. Let her take one copy to school each day. At the end of the day, ask your child to draw something that happened to her and her favorite animal. You can write the words if she isn't ready to manage that part of the task. All the pages can go together in a notebook that will make a series of personal adventures.

A child who is feeling emotionally wistful—or disengaged from school for emotional reasons—will find this activity enjoyable and reassuring. The child who feels insignificant will feel more powerful in the role of host and protector of a beloved creature.

3. Bait the trap with suspense. "In three days, I'm going to teach you something most kids don't learn until they're older." When the big day comes, produce a limerick; a "witcrack" such as, "One bright morning in the middle of the night, two dead boys got up to fight . . ." or "Last winter, a cow nearby caught such a cold she gave nothing but ice cream"; or the mnemonic device for remembering the names of the Great Lakes (HOMES: Huron, Ontario, Michigan, Erie, Superior). The content matters much less than the suspense and your child's sense that he is being let in on a big kids' secret.

Three-Dimensional or Two-Dimensional

1. Make opportunities for your child to translate her social studies book learning into table-top demonstrations and models. The materials may be elaborate or simple. While a 4' x 6' piece of fiberboard astride two tables is a grand-scale opportunity, shoebox dioramas work well, too. The point is that a little bit of paint, some clay, dental floss tied to a toothpick for a fishing line, a drinking straw as the tent pole for a dwelling, bits of brown paper bag cut to look like hide being tanned, and other bits and pieces of household detritus can give your 3-D child a chance to show knowledge, have fun, and feel competent.

2. Play Feely Bag. Gather six or seven common objects: a cassette, a spoon, an eraser, a button, a spool of thread, a felt-tip pen, a bottle of Wite-Out. Give your child a chance to hold, feel, squeeze, sniff, and generally become familiar with the objects' properties. Then remove all of the objects from the room, and while you're out of view, close your eyes, choose one object, and drop it in the Feely Bag. Bring the Feely Bag back into the room, put a hand in it, and describe the object *by properties only.* From hearing clues of size, shape, texture, and weight, your child must try to figure out which object it is. Choose some objects with overlapping properties to make the activity more difficult.

3. Second graders are ripe for science projects. A simple way to launch your 3-D child is to start a leaf collection. Let her collect, identify, label, mount, and categorize. After the exhibit has been put together using one set of categories, can she think of another way to group the materials? Have your child make a grouping and articulate the rule. Science has a playful, exploratory dimension that is sometimes stifled.

Simultaneous or Sequential

1. Surveys and graphs are ideal vehicles for your second-grade child. Whether he is polling for numbers of lost teeth, color preferences, or favorite foods, he will enjoy the physical act of roaming around, his natural nosiness finds appropriate outlet in investigative reporting, and graphing the results unites simultaneous and sequential thinking.

2. Together with your child, make a Compound Word Ribbon. Cut pieces of $8\frac{1}{2}''$ x $11''$ paper in half lengthwise and join the pieces end to end. Write all the compound words your child can think of. For example, she might come up with *school yard, hot dog, upside-down,* or *farmhouse.* Tape the ribbon on the top of her bedroom wall, rec room, or other appropriate location, and tell your child the goal is to wrap the ribbon all the way around the wall. Each day, have your child try to think of new contributions.

3. A Person of the Week easel or board allows your child to think, say, write, and draw about someone in the world or local news. You, as the parent, say, "Every Monday morning I will put five clues on the easel. You have until bedtime to figure out the new Person of the Week. Your opportunity between Monday and Thursday is to write or draw one reason this person is special and a good choice. We will attach your comments to my clues, and celebrate the Person of the Week on Friday."

Multisensory

- visual
- auditory
- kinesthetic/tactile

Visual

1. Read your child a story—or use a story she has read herself—and ask her to make a five-frame or ten-frame cartoon of the narrative.

2. Keep a big calendar (showing several months at a time, but with generous spaces to annotate the events of each day) in a highly visible location such as the bedroom, homework space, or refrigerator. At the end of each day, ask your child to draw a little rebus showing something that happened that day. In advance, mark important events: the class play, the science fair, a birthday party. Ask questions as a way of solidifying a time line in your child's mind:

"How many days in the last two weeks has it rained?"

"How many boys in your class had birthdays last month?"

"How many girls?"

"Is there any day of the week that has more birthdays than the other six?"

"How many weeks until you visit your cousins?"

"Are you more or less than halfway through second grade?"

"Tell me something that happened last week on the day between Monday and Wednesday."

Remember that time is an invisible concept, accessible only through language. You provide that access when you offer your child a visual, sequential, annotated accompaniment to this abstract concept.

3. Play Sight-Word Concentration. Explain to your child that there are many words we simply recognize without stopping to sound them out; these are sight words. The combination of a good supply of sight words and solid grounding in phonics makes reading easier and more pleasurable. So, he'll learn his phonics, and at the same time he'll boost his sight-word vocabulary.

Take a list of fifteen sight words, thirty colored index cards, and write each word on two cards, making a set of fifteen pairs. (Choose your sight words from the list of 220 Dolch Basic Sight Words in appendix B.) Shuffle the cards, spread them out face down, and play for the collection of pairs, following the procedure for Concentration.

For those of you who need a brief refresher course on the game, player one turns two cards face up. If those two cards are a matching pair, he gets to keep both cards and take another turn; if he doesn't find the pair, he must turn both cards face down, and player two then takes a turn. The same process is repeated for player two. The goal is to remember the location of each card so that when its mate is turned over, the player whose turn it is can make a match and keep the cards. The player with the most pairs at the end of the game wins.

Auditory

1. Play I Spy with My Little Eye, teaching your child to visualize the clues as she hears them. For example, if you select the plant on the windowsill in the kitchen, say "I spy with my little eye something green." Your child must ask only questions

that can be answered yes or no until she has the answer. As with the numbers game referred to for younger children, your child will learn to—or you can help her to—ask winnowing and harvesting questions, instead of buckshot random ones: "Is it in the front half of the room?" "Is it bigger than a breadbox?" (Am I giving away my age by using that question?)

Obviously, in order to narrow down to the object, your child must keep an increasingly refined collection of mental images set in place by what she has heard. This is excellent practice for focused listening.

2. Read aloud to your child, asking him to make mental movies as the story goes along. (Refer back to the comments on audiotapes for family trips in the General Principles of Good Practice section on page 51).

3. Use Scrabble tiles (or any other alphabet tiles that you have around the home) and types of syllables written out on slips of paper to make Nonsense Words with your child. Second graders particularly enjoy playing with mythical inventions. Marcus, a second-grade California child, drew the letters and syllables to make the word *Pet-scan-a-roo*. His definition read, "A wrist device like a watch. When you put the face towards a person, a picture of their pet automatically appears." Well, *petscanaroo* is a pretty long word for a second grader to decode, but those who are playing with syllables on slips of paper—and whose humor is simultaneously engaged—manage very well. And, by the way, I wear my Dick Tracy petscanaroo every day, don't you?

Kinesthetic/Tactile

1. Stand behind your child, and with the pointing finger of your writing hand, draw a letter on her back. At the beginning, simply ask your child to provide the sound/symbol corre-spondence. As she progresses, ask her first for a word start-ing with that sound, then a word ending with that sound.

2. Measure the World. Your second grader will feel a sense of power and competence in taking, recording, and clas-sifying the dimensions of his everyday surroundings. To set your second-grade child off on missions of measur-ing the length or width of his bedroom, the front hall, and the size of the kitchen compared with the size of the garage, is to set a thinker loose on a journey of compar-ative calculations. Isn't that what most fulfilled adults are doing?

3. Collect a list of emotions from your child. You may want to use alphabetical order to get the juices flowing. Write them on a piece of paper. Then, without looking at the list, point to one of the words. Ask your child to look at the word and think about the ramifications of that emotion, and then act it out. For instance, suppose the word was *rage*. Have your child make the face a person experiencing rage would be likely to make, then get up and walk in a cir-cle using the posture and gait a person experiencing rage would be likely to exhibit. Of course, this is closely con-nected to other exercises in pretending mentioned earlier and later.

Eager to Make Connections

- filing
- retrieving
- recombining

1. Be sure to teach time. Because digital watches are readily and inexpensively available to young—and even very young—

children, it is easy for adults to mistake the easy number-calling from a dial for the actual understanding of time.

Here's a way to teach telling time from the face of a clock. On a paper plate write the hour numbers in green. On the outside rim, write the minute numbers in five-minute increments in red. From cardboard, make and cut two clock hands—the short in green, the long in red. Fasten them at the center of the paper plate with a brad.

Tell your child that the green hand reads the green numbers, the red hand reads the red numbers. The little hand, color-coded green for go, always "speaks" first.

2. Ask your child to select his two favorite stuffed animals. Create a shoebox for each animal with a cover made from plastic wrap and (black paper) bars. Put each stuffed animal inside just such a no-exit shoebox, and ask your child to write a description of each animal. Agree beforehand on the categories and specifics to be described (which is actually a preliminary exercise to Zoology 105), such as what type of climate each animal is likely accustomed to, what kind of food they each eat, their habitats, and whether they are domesticated animals or ones that roam free in the environment.

3. After each animal is categorized, ask your child to describe each individual animal, then how the animals are similar and different, then what would happen if they were to meet, and then what would happen if these two animals—as a team—were to run into another pair of animals that you have selected. The opportunities for imaginative speculation and refinement of thinking are limited only by you and your child's imaginations.

Gifted, Precocious, or Just Plain Smart

- factual
- aesthetic
- imaginary

1. Hang an "I Am Proud of . . ." bulletin board or poster in a public spot in your home. When your child does something particularly well, or tells a great joke, or does extra work caring for the family pet, suggest that she write a sentence or two about it and put it on the bulletin board. There is a great difference between boastfulness and acknowledging personal competence. Your child needs legitimate outlets for telling what she is proud of.

2. Ask your child to choose and memorize a poem. Then ask him to make a cover showing the title, and inside copy the poem in his best handwriting and illustrate it. Ask your child to recite his poem to you and other family members, and pass the book around for everyone to see.

3. Explore new interests with your child. Your child should nominate topics; they shouldn't be chosen only by you. Topics to be explored can range widely: Exploring Arctic Animals to Magic Tricks to Math Mavens to Writing a Family Newsletter. (Far-flung grandparents, or even grandparents who live around the block, will be enthusiastic readers—or subscribers.) For some topics, you will simply need to set out the materials, and your child can move on from there. For others, you might need help from a librarian or the Internet to find the materials and perhaps give an introductory lesson. But the emphasis should not be on direct, lecture-style teaching. The real purpose is to spread some tempting examples or ideas before your child, and then stand back and see what she can do on her own.

CHAPTER 11

THIRD GRADE

Curriculum Overview

In third grade, the emphasis shifts from "learning to read" to "reading to learn." Even the neurological process is different. As Richard Masland, M.D., past president of the World Federation of Neurology, points out, early reading is a process of pattern recognition. At third grade, reading changes into a process of linguistic recognition.

The child who has a deep pool of internal language from which to draw will readily recognize rhythms, cadence, shadings, and subtleties, and will be able to "cast a linguistic shadow"—to anticipate the writer's next words.

The linguistically nimble child will read with comprehension, which includes establishing the setting and sequence of the plot, being able to gather information from print, identifying with characters' behaviors and feelings, and making inferences.

These capacities are not limited to what happens in reading class, but apply across the curriculum. In math, word problems join language with numbers; in social studies, understanding depends on good vocabulary and a solid supply of general information. On the playground, in the hall, and in the lunchroom, third-grade badinage relies on puns, gleeful insults, and the lingo of "in" jokes.

Students who have trouble with figurative language need to be liberated from concrete thinking by being taught that one word can have more than one meaning—by being exposed to homophones (*steal/steel*), homographs (*present/present*), synonyms (*damp/moist*), antonyms (*hot/cold*), simile (*as pretty as* . . .), metaphor (*He was my anchor*), proverbs (*Two heads are better than one*), and figures of speech (*bullheaded*).

This is the real job and curriculum of third grade. Subject matter is a vehicle for—and expression of—language development. Strong linguistic foundations give your child a solid base on which to build lifelong learning. Weakness here will be debilitating and inconvenient at this age, and like the unseen work of termites, will bore holes through information and undermine conceptual foundations, replacing substance with sawdust!

Word-retrieval problems, described on pages 36 and 37, will have a pernicious effect, particularly on written work.

Practical Suggestions for Six Learning Patterns

Available for Schoolwork

- physically
- emotionally
- intellectually

1. Your third-grade child is ready to learn some fundamentals of physiology. Make four charts and head them "Diet," "Sleep," "Hygiene," "General Health." Draw a line down the center of each to form a plus column and a minus col-

umn. Ask your child to brainstorm elements of a healthy diet and elements of unhealthy eating habits. Then ask your child to write about one food that is healthy and tempting, and another which is tempting and unhealthy. When your child has finished, help him make a list of some other foods that are healthy and tempting, and another list for foods that are tempting and unhealthy. Discuss with your child: What elements do unhealthy foods have in common? Healthy foods? Which cost more? Which kind gets more advertising?

Use this format to explore sleep habits, good and poor personal hygiene, and general health.

2. Find a way for your child to have some responsibility for another living creature. Grow grass on potato halves, grow plants from avocado pits, grow shoots from lima beans, keep a fish tank in your home, have a pet if there are no allergies in the family. Through the act of bestowing care, your child will build strong connections to life around her.

3. Make a Language Expansion Chart on a piece of paper. At the top, write a simple sentence or sentence fragment. Over several weeks, encourage your child to find richer, more interesting ways of saying the same thing.

For example, you might start with "He went . . ." Your child might come up with such alternatives as he *galloped,* he *traveled,* he *lunged,* he *journeyed,* he *ambled,* he *strode,* he *sidestepped his way,* he *vaulted,* he *slithered,* he *snuck,* he *tiptoed.*

When this chart is full, make another one involving any of the following language development categories: synonyms, antonyms, homophones, homographs, similes, metaphors, proverbs, figures of speech.

Three-Dimensional or Two-Dimensional

1. Collector's Showcase. Set up a corner of a room as a mini-museum. Ask your child to exhibit a favorite collection of his. Ask your exhibitor to give an overview of the scope and purpose of the collection in a brief (ten-sentence) talk to the audience (you and/or additional family members). Have him point out to the audience what he has collected, why the items are grouped as they are, what is special. Family members should be given an opportunity to study the exhibit and ask questions of the exhibitor.

2. Read T. S. Eliot's *Old Possum's Book of Practical Cats* aloud to your child. Play the videotape of the show *Cats*. Then ask your child to think up a brand-new cat. Describe it, draw it, name it, or make a model of it.

3. Come up with a list of questions to ask your child about the newly minted cat: Where does it live? What does it like to do? What are its favorite foods? What kind of trouble does it get into? How does it get along with humans? Your cat creator should answer each of these questions either by drawing, by describing, or by showing in a model.

Simultaneous or Sequential

1. If you want to banish winter doldrums and still have plenty of opportunities for your child to practice and reinforce decoding, word recognition, and language development, Madame Marvella, the Fortune-Teller is for you. This favorite schoolroom activity can be done easily at home.

Madame Marvella, the Fortune-Teller

One February, I decided we needed something new to chase away the winter boredom, and invented a fortune-telling game that swept throughout the school. I started with a poster (see below) to tempt participants and to explain the components. Since this activity was designed to provide practice in following directions, as well as to stretch vocabulary and to enliven midwinter, I made a Chart of Directions explaining how to proceed (see pages 96-98). The students could do this completely on their own. In addition, I dittoed a Fortune Sheet for each student to use in recording his results (see page 99).

Put the Chart of Directions where your child can see it, and spread out the necessary props (the die, the cards, the Personality Fishbowl containers, the Color Scheme chart, and the Alphabet Board or open book). Give your child his own Fortune Sheet to fill out, keep, and compare.

MADAME MARVELLA, THE FORTUNE-TELLER

See the Future! Discover the Secrets of Your Personality!

1. Alphabet Clue
2. Nice Dice
3. Pick a Card
4. Personality Fishbowl
5 Color Scheme
6. What's Next

Chart of Directions

1. **Alphabet Clue:** If the last letter of your first name is in the first half of the alphabet, consider yourself outstanding. If it is in the last half of the alphabet, consider yourself a national treasure.

2. **Nice Dice.** Roll the dice three times. Add the numbers together for your total. The total is the number of your wishes that will come true. If your total is an even number, they will come true quickly. If it is an odd number, they will come true slowly.

3. **Pick a Card.** Cards come in four suits:

spades

hearts

diamonds

clubs

Pick a card from the deck to learn about your work habits.

If you draw a **spade,** your work habits are *orderly.*

If you draw a **heart**, they are *magnificent.*

If you draw a **diamond**, they are *sparkling.*

If you draw a **club**, they are *steady.*

4. **Personality Fishbowl.** Draw two cards from the bowl. These words describe how you usually are. Draw one slip from the cup. Since no one is perfect all the time, it describes how you sometimes are. Please replace the slips.

Suggested Word Lists for the Personality Fishbowl

FISHBOWL WORDS **CUP WORDS**

independent	generous	disorganized
helpful	musical	caterwauling
witty	unselfish	overwhelming
effervescent	reliable	bullheaded
exhilarating	spontaneous	devious
amiable	team-spirited	ornery
friendly	unique	pugnacious
ebullient	gorgeous	willful
optimistic	spectacular	uncooperative
fabulous	gregarious	bombastic
honest	consistent	stubborn
fair	courteous	balky
courageous	benevolent	reluctant
sunny	remarkable	lazy
delightful	artistic	recalcitrant
fantastic	even-tempered	messy
intelligent	open-minded	noisy
sensational	brave	fresh
marvelous	gentle	outrageous

5. Color Scheme. Choose your favorite color and consult the color scheme list to see what it reveals about your energy level.

red . . . . *vigorous*

orange . . . . *high*

yellow . . . . *consistent*

green . . . . *variable*

blue . . . . *unpredictable*

purple . . . . *highest in the morning*

brown . . . . *highest at night*

black . . . . *low until lunch*

white . . . . *astonishing*

6. What's Next? Close your eyes and put your finger on a letter of the alphabet, using the Alphabet Board or any open book. Below, find the word beginning with that letter to describe your future.

a: assured

b: beautiful

c: contented

d: delicious

e: excellent

f: fancy

g: gorgeous

h: happy

i: inspired

j: jocose

k: keen

l: lovely

m: momentous

n: notable

o: opulent

p: pretty

qu: quick-witted

r: racy

s: stellar

t: terrific

u: unbelievable

v: venerable

w: wonderful

x: (e)xciting

y: yummy

z: zippy

Congratulations!

Fortune Sheet

Name _____

Date _____

1. Alphabet Clue tells me that I am

_____.

2. Nice Dice tells me that_____

    wishes will come true quickly slowly.

3. Pick a Card tells me that my work habits are

_____.

4. Personality Fishbowl tells me that I am usually

_____, and _____,

but sometimes I am _____.

5. Color Scheme tells me that my energy level is

_____.

6. What's Next tells me that my future looks

_____.

Hooray!

2. Help your child make up new word lists for each Madame Marvella category.

3. Together with your child, chart and categorize other forms of fortune-telling she may have heard of—such as cards, horoscopes, tea leaves, phrenology, palm readings, and prophetic verses such as "Monday's child is fair of face"— and ask her to tell you whether she thinks fortune telling is a) reliable, and/or b) enjoyable.

Multisensory

- visual
- auditory
- kinesthetic/tactile

Visual

1. Time Lines. As I have mentioned, time is an abstract concept accessible only through language. Many children also need a visual accompaniment. Ask your child to turn a piece of $8\frac{1}{2}''$ x $11''$ paper horizontally. Draw a line from left to right. At the center of the line, put a blue dot to indicate the present. Moving leftward from that dot, draw a red horizontal line; moving to the right, draw a green line. Red will be the past—no new growth possible. Green will be the future.

Start with simple common experience. How old are you now? Help your child write that number over the blue dot. Then have have him count backward to his birth, putting dots at even intervals. Ask him what he or the family did the year he was one. Did you move? Did he learn to walk? What did he do on his birthday? Do the same for each year in the past, helping your child jot words or small pictures at each age. Now have him count off the same number of years into the future. Ask him what he hopes he will do next year, when he is twelve, etc.

2. Ask your child to make a graph of the distribution of birthdays for the family (including grandparents, aunts, uncles, cousins) and her friends across the calendar year. Display the results.

3. Make and display a chart of the six types of syllables (listed below). Have your child name and draw an animal to illustrate each one:

Six Types of Syllables

closed syllable (cvc) . . . .*cat*
open syllable (cv) . . . . *ti-ger*
silent *e* . . . . *mule*
vowel team . . . . *deer*
r-controlled . . . . *shark*
bird
worm
horse
herd
consonant plus *le* . . . . *tur-tle*

Auditory

1. Accent is more than a food spice. Accents tell us which parts of a word to emphasize, and help us pronounce words correctly. For instance, try *say-ing syll-able* with the accents on the ends of the words instead of at the beginning. You will sound like a foreigner reading from a guidebook. Your third grader is ready to begin accent analysis. Say a word, ask your child to tell you which syllable has the accent, then ask her to try to say the word accenting a different syllable. Here are a few words to fool around with: *calendar, Thanksgiving, musical, automobile, radio, microwave,* *pencil, countertop.* For fun, try animals: *elephant, zebra, tiger, hippopotamus, crocodile.* Vegetables and fruits also work well for these purposes: *zucchini, banana, cantaloupe, avocado.*

2. Use your child's natural facility with learning songs to help him memorize. Set the multiplication tables to music. In my own family, I discovered that the 4's table fits "The Star-Spangled Banner" ("Four times one equals four, four times two equals eight, four times three i-is twelve, four times four is sixtee-en," etc.) Pavarotti it's not, but for a kid who has trouble memorizing combinations, it's a godsend. "My Darling Clementine" works well for the 7's table ("Seven ones they come to seven, seven twos are fourteen, seven threes are twenty-one, seven fours are twenty-eight").

3. Continue counting and analyzing syllables. Give your child a word, ask her to hold up as many fingers as there are syllables in the word. Then ask her to say or spell a particular syllable. For example, "Your word is *cucumber.* That's right, three syllables. Pronounce and spell the second syllable. Good."

Kinesthetic/Tactile

1. Make Disguised Letter Pictures. Choose a letter, write it in yellow on a piece of paper. Now try to incorporate that letter shape in a picture of an object. Use as many other colors as you like for the object. Can your child find the letter *s* in the sample?

2. Maintain handwriting instruction. Use only one manual system. If the school still uses two systems, and your child has a hard time converting, let him stay with his preference. This right is worth fighting for.

3. Teach or learn the Cat's Cradle and other string games. The combination of pattern, sequence, and foolishness is a joy to children this age. Children who shine in this area will enjoy macramé.

Eager to Make Connections

- filing
- retrieving
- recombining

1. Use Red Pen Traffic Lights to show your kid how to read, understand, and follow directions. "When you see a set of directions, get out your red pen. Scan across the direction until you see the first period. Put a red line under it. Continue scanning to the next, put in a red line, scan to the next, put in a red line. When you have scanned the directions, count the number of red lines and put a corresponding number of marks at the top of the page.

"Read as far as the first red line. It is a traffic light. STOP. See in your mind's eye what you are being told to do. Once you understand this segment, cross off one of the marks at the top of the page and proceed to the next traffic light. STOP. Visualize what you are to do. Cross off the second mark at the top of the page. Continue in this way until you have crossed off all the marks at the top of the page.

"Now read the directions through from the beginning and do as they say."

2. Practice estimating elapsing time. "Look up at the time now. Look up again when you think ten minutes have passed. Check your guess. We'll do this every day until you get good at keeping track of time while you're working. This will help you when you are writing a pop quiz or five-minute creative writing sample in class. It will help you keep track of yourself doing your homework. Later on, when you take exams, you will thank me for having taught you this."

3. Using alphabetical order, invent a roster of imaginary foods with your child. Third graders enjoy the rhythm and rumble of nonsense words. One group produced: *agalops, blerps, catkine, denk, effluts, foozle, gratz, hitslop, immidge, jalooka, kroft, lumpola, manfree, nelligud, opura, pripadoodle, querp, rast, slig, tarm, utch, vame, wizzle, xerphane, yergle,* and *zard.* A list such as this makes an excellent reading and spelling checkup. Nonsense words catch weaknesses and pinpoint uncertainties.

Once the list exists, choose several words and ask your child to think up definitions.

Gifted, Precocious, or Just Plain Smart

- factual
- aesthetic
- imaginary

1. Design a board game with your child. Use a manila file folder, put the title on the cover, and draw the path on the inside.

Your child will need to decide whether it is a word recognition/reading game, a numbers game, or an information game. Then she needs to draw out the path, decide how many of the spaces to use for obstacles/perils (You forgot to make your bed. Miss one turn.), and plan what artwork should represent the "Home" spot. It could be a pot of gold, a spot on TV, a food feast, or whatever strikes her fancy.

The title, the illustrations around the path, and the

Home spot should all represent the same theme. Reminder: The path should start in the upper left-hand corner and make its way to the lower right.

Play your child's invention.

2. Try to combine different age groups and talents in designing and producing new games. Give them chances to appreciate one another's talents and to benefit from one another's expertise. This is an ideal vehicle for grandparents and grandchildren.

3. Machinimagination. Ask your child to collect a plastic bag of household throwaway items (dry only, please). Have him put them together to make a machine from his imagination. Help your child write out a user's manual, describing function, procedures, dangers, and what to do in case of malfunction. The creator should indicate probable price and outline an advertising campaign.

CHAPTER 12

FOURTH GRADE

Curriculum Overview

The fourth grader's mind vaults to new levels of complexity and understanding. Ideas come on a flood tide, and the brighter the child, the more there is to channel. For this reason, many fourth graders have trouble organizing what they hear, what they read, what they say, and what they write. Many have trouble with exercises in workbooks or grade-normed readers which exhort them to "find the main idea." All ideas seem like main ideas, because whole new ways of recognizing connections open up.

By fourth grade, most students have developed an easy, rhythmic handwriting that allows their hands to keep pace with their thoughts. Children who have not reached this level of "kinetic melody" are at high risk for academic problems. It is vital to train this skill to a comfortable level, because during this year—and ever thereafter—trouble from this area spreads a stain across the student's total academic output.

While handwriting is a subsidiary rather than primary subject, its effect on school achievement, self-concept, and willingness to risk is enormous.

This is the year to teach accurate keyboard fingering to children with poor handwriting. For reasons mentioned previously, it is false assistance to simply turn them loose on a word processor, developing their idiosyncratic hunt-and peck systems, which will be difficult to unlearn later in favor of efficient keyboard skills. In my experience, other children can wait until early fifth grade for keyboarding lessons and will pick it up very quickly, because there is a good developmental match between hand size, muscle memory, and a keyboard.

For children who memorize readily, this is a vintage year. Things just stick. The danger is that accurate recitation can mask underlying conceptual confusion, particularly in math. Fourth graders need to continue using manipulatives, and they need to write their math concepts out in paragraphs or essay form, as well as do computation laid out for them by the teacher.

Children who struggle to memorize their math facts need to use design and color to draw the progression of the multiplication tables, they need to sing the songs associated with the tables (see page 102), and they need to be given time to think out answers they cannot spout. Around the World and Mad Minute games are torture to such students and reinforce the paralytic links joining math, fear, and failure.

In the classroom, the fourth grader is by turns empathic and critical. Children this age can be taught to be tolerant of differences, though they probably wouldn't be so on their own. Underneath still childishly plump cheeks, hormones are beginning to race, and bodily changes are around the corner.

As they sense their own bodies changing, many boys become hyperconscious of their own and others' physical coordination and athletic skills. The jock is "in"; the nerd is exiled.

Thanks to hormones, many girls need to wash their hair

more frequently and use deodorant. The tomboy who isn't aware of her need may be scorned as a baby, and one whose development comes early seems like a foreigner.

Along with this rapid-transit shuttle back and forth between childhood and early adolescence comes a powerful, new intellectual capacity: Fourth graders can hold two conflicting ideas in their minds simultaneously and reason their way through ambiguity. This capacity allows them to play simulation games with verve and skill. They are also ripe for cooperative learning, as well as for individual reasoning.

In working with your fourth-grade child, you (and your child's teachers) must be certain that the levels of language development described in the last chapter are firmly and crisply in place. The internal time line should be solid, allowing your child to read narratives in sequence, understand flashbacks, and sort social and historical events into periods.

Practical Suggestions for Six Learning Patterns

Available for Schoolwork

- physically
- emotionally
- intellectually

1. Help your child explore some of the somatic conditions that influence availability. Ask your child to write out and then complete the sentence, "When I'm sleepy, I . . ."

Follow the same procedure for, "When I'm hungry, I . . ." By helping your kid call attention to her own bodily sensations, you help her recognize them. This is the first step to anticipating "what I might feel like if I don't get enough sleep, protein, etc."

2. Russell Hoban must have had fourth graders in mind when he wrote *How Tom Beat Captain Najork and His Hired Sportsmen,* the story of a hapless boy named Tom, who has the bad luck to live in the custody of Aunt Fidget Wonkham-Strong, who wears an iron hat, serves him greasy bloaters and mutton sog, and requires him to memorize pages of the nautical almanac. Tom likes to fool around instead. Aunt Fidget Wonkham-Strong sends for her friend Captain Najork and his hired sportsmen to teach Tom a thing or two. They challenge the boy at such mythical games as Muck and Sneedball. Because of all his contraband practice at fooling around, Tom defeats them handily. And the denouement will remain a mystery here. Turn fourth-grade imaginations loose by letting them read the book and then invent new games for the hired sportsmen, or for Tom to use in a return challenge.

Fourth graders' natural interest in games, rules, scoring, and equipment makes this an ideal way to engage their humor and their inventiveness. This book is out of print, but you can check your local library or a used bookstore to find a copy for your child; or use the principle of the story to play with the idea.

3. By fourth grade your child will be old enough to learn the difference between simile and metaphor. Experiment first with simile. For example, you might approach the topic by dumping the contents of your pocketbook or briefcase out on a table and saying to your child, "Pick up one of the things from my purse, and make me an original simile." Your child might come up with, "a glove as soft as cotton," "a wallet as worn as an old woman's smile," "a coin as shiny silver as the moon," or "a lipstick case as hard and shiny as a rocket."

Then explain, "A simile pairs ideas with each other, but a metaphor makes a statement, which—although symbolic—is single. For example, taking some of your similes, I might say, 'You are the shiny silver moon of my sky,' or 'Dad is the rocket of our family discussions.'

"Select three objects or perceptions, and write them on an index card first as similes. Then, on the reverse side write them as metaphors."

Three-Dimensional or Two-Dimensional

1. Ask your child what associations she has for the word *star*. The group of fourth graders I worked with recently thought of *Star Wars*; "Star light, star bright, first star I see tonight"; being a movie or TV star; "seeing stars," as in getting punched; the military designation of four-star general; the Star of David; the nativity star; "Stars and Stripes Forever"; Venus, the evening star; and getting a star on your paper, homework, or test. The collection represented both the benevolent and destructive sides of human nature, with a little mystery and romance thrown in.

   Next, read aloud the first three quarters of *The Little Prince*, by Antoine de Saint-Exupéry, relishing the whimsy and beautiful language, and noticing how many different kinds of stars he describes having met on his journey to earth.

   Then help your child invent a brand-new star. Would it be large, small, hostile, friendly, etc.?

2. Brainstorm with your child what kinds of questions it would be important to ask if someone invited you to come and visit the new stars. Here are some from my group: How do I get there? Can I get back? Is there air? Is there water? What is the climate? Are the inhabitants like us? How are

they different? What kind of communication system is there? What about doctors and medical care? What kind of currency do they use? Are there many species? What kinds of dwellings are there? Is there government or law? What is the entertainment? What are the activities and sports? What are some of their rituals? What are the taboos? From this group came a profusion of intelligent, thoughtful questions which—on reflection—are the outline for Anthropology 105!

Make sure your child includes information on all the above topics, as well as others she finds interesting. Ask your child to write a poem about her star, and say that she can give additional information about her star by creating maps, models, a display of artifacts, a census, a written description, a travel brochure, an advertisement, or a warning. The only limits are those set by your child's imagination.

When the work is completed, read from the concluding section of *The Little Prince*. Here the prince explains that it is time for him to return whence he came. But he assures his friend that he will be casting a benevolent, mirthful eye down upon him. He says that other people will see silent stars, but that his friend will have the stars that can laugh.

Suggest to your child that perhaps she has changed her own view of the nighttime heavens forever. Whenever she looks up, she may be looking for the star of her own invention. You might even want to cover a bulletin board or other flat surface with midnight blue construction paper, make a heading of e. e. cummings's line "in the street of the sky night walked scattering poems," and hang your child's star poem.

3. Finally, ask your child to design a transportation network connecting the star with Earth. Make sure she includes

speed, expense, fuel, construction, number of passengers, safety guidelines, and whether it would be run by humans, remote control, or automatically.

Joy, imagination, energy, information, cooperation, creativity, and pride combine to make this a 3-D/2-D showcase.

Simultaneous or Sequential

1. To mark the conclusion of one of your child's social studies units, help her put together an exhibit showing what she has learned. Have your child describe and explain her exhibit to you or other family members.

2. Select a story your child probably has not heard before. Read three quarters of it aloud. Then ask your child to anticipate the author's ending and write a different one. Ask your child to share the suggested alternate ending, and then read what the author actually wrote.

3. Select a story your child probably hasn't heard and tell him he is going to be asked to convert it into a play. Read it aloud and ask him to convert it to a theater, radio, or TV script.

Multisensory

- visual
- auditory
- kinesthetic/tactile

Visual

1. Have a large calendar—preferably showing several months at a time—hung in full view. Decide with your child what types of events are important to anticipate (the class play,

tests, soccer practices, soccer games, school assemblies, etc.), give a color to each one, and color code the calendar together. This is important and appropriate for every grade, so don't think this implies regression simply because younger children have used the same exercise.

2. The concept of baseball cards can help your fourth-grade child codify, classify, and chart characters from the literature she is reading, or people or events from history or social studies. A pack of colored index cards works beautifully. Your child draws a picture of the person on the front and writes relevant information on the back.

For example, if your child is studying folktales and fairy tales, she might have one pack per story. Snow White's pack would have a card apiece for Snow White, the wicked queen, the huntsman, each of the dwarves, and Prince Charming. Your child would decide in advance on the information grid that would unify the pack. In this case, it might be title of story, name of character, major character traits, physical appearance, role in story, characters in other stories who play similar roles, and three adjectives giving your child's reaction to the character.

3. Fourth graders like to play with words—inventing and dismantling them. Get three pieces of poster board or paper. In green for go, title the first "Prefixes." In brown for tree roots, title the second "Roots." In red for stop, title the third "Suffixes." With your child—and using the corresponding color pen—brainstorm and write a collection for each category. Then see how many existing words your child can make from the selection on display, and how many new words he can invent using these same building blocks.

For example, one group learned that the suffix *itis* refers to inflammation. They talked about tonsillitis, appendicitis, arthritis, and so forth.

Auditory

1. Fourth graders who are learning—and, hopefully, applying—spelling rules need to maintain their awareness of long and short vowel discrimination. Why? Roughly 75 percent of spelling rules depend on knowing whether the vowel is long or short. Help your child review long and short vowels.

Say, "I'll say a word to you at breakfast (or dinner). If it has a long vowel, draw a horizontal line in the air. Such words might be *lake, bean, pine, cone, cute.* If it has a short vowel, draw a 'scoop' (u) in the air." Such words might be *ask, wedge, pinch, hot, bum.*

Once your child is comfortable identifying long and short vowels, review more complex vowel discrimination with them. For example, you might say, "Do you use *ge* or *dge?* Long vowels take *ge*, some examples include *stage* and *huge.* Short vowels take *dge*; for example, *badge, wedge, ridge, lodge,* and *fudge.* Do you double the consonant when adding a suffix? In a one-syllable word with one short vowel and one final consonant, you double the final consonant when adding a suffix, so *run* becomes *running,* and *stop* becomes *stopping.* You do not double the final consonant if the vowel is long—*smile* becomes *smiling*—or when there is more than one consonant at the end—*stand* becomes *standing.*"

The point is that understanding spelling rules depends on vowel discrimination, which is generally taught in kindergarten and first grade but is considered beneath the lofty appetites of older students.

2. Many of today's children are nostalgic for their own child-hoods. They don't dare appear babyish, but they often hunger for stuffed animals and picture books. Dignify this yearning by asking your child to choose three or four of his favorite childhood stories, practice reading them aloud, and then record them for younger children.

3. Teach your child mnemonic devices for memorizing. As mentioned in the second-grade section, HOMES is an acronym for the names of the Great Lakes (Huron, Ontario, Michigan, Erie, and Superior). The phrase "Washington ate jam merrily merrily" gives the first letter of the last names of the first five presidents (Washington, Adams, Jefferson, Madison, Monroe). Your fourth grader will find it both amusing and productive to catalogue her knowledge in this way.

Kinesthetic/Tactile

1. For reasons mentioned earlier, fourth graders need con-tinuing instruction and practice in handwriting. Rather than finding the repetition onerous, most find it soothing. Provide opportunities for your child to practice his hand-writing at home.

2. Routinely ask your child to write out the alphabet in lower case, then in upper case. This takes less than a minute to complete.

3. "An elephant madly squirts" is the mnemonic device for breaking the dictionary into quarters. The faster your child knows where to start looking for a word, the more quickly she will find it. When your child can find words quickly, she won't avoid looking them up.

Here's how it works. No matter the weight of the paper

or size of the print, *M* is generally at the middle of the book. Open the book to the middle. Letters that follow *M* will be called the "after half"; letters preceding *M* are the "before half." The middle of the "before half" generally falls at *E*; the middle of the "after half" at *S*.

Begin practicing by naming a letter and having your child say whether it comes in the before or after half. Then concentrate on the before half. Give a word; your child must decide whether its first letter comes before or after *E*. Let him practice finding words in those first two quarters of the book. Then proceed in the same way with the second half of the book. Then, use the whole book, reminding your child to ask himself, "Before or after *M*?", then "Before or after *E*?", "Before or after *S*?"

Eager to Make Connections

- filing
- retrieving
- recombining

1. The National Council of Teachers of Mathematics has endorsed the use of calculators for students in fourth grade and above. Children who have trouble memorizing math combinations will find this a great relief, but it is one that too often becomes a mirage. Unless your child has a strong sense of logic—a logic alarm system—she has no way of being sure of having pressed the correct keys. Those who reverse letter sequence in reading or spelling are prone to the same errors with numerals. The kid who taps in 71 instead of 17 on his calculator will get an incorrect result and not know why.

   Help your child protect herself with an automatic logic alarm by giving her exercises in estimation. For example,

"If you go to the supermarket and buy ten items ranging in price from 75 to 99 cents, will you have spent a) more than ten dollars, b) around ten dollars, c) considerably under ten dollars?"

2. Over the Rainbow. Each of us has personal associations for colors. Fourth graders enjoy sharing their own perceptions and emotions, and this is a noninvasive way to get your fourth grader going. Give your child a piece of construction paper in each of the six colors of the spectrum. Superimpose a piece of unlined white paper, trimmed by 1 inch on each side. The colored paper will look like a frame. Then ask him to take a pen in that color and write, "Red reminds me of . . ." Ask your child to write at least ten associations for each color. When he is done, join all the pieces together with a cover sheet, which can be titled *Over the Rainbow* and illustrated as ornately as taste dictates.

3. Lexicon Switch provides language experimentation in a way that tickles fourth graders. Learning to categorize words that are frequently used together in different types of written or spoken genres, your child expands her linguistic sensitivities. Begin by brainstorming with your child about some of the lexicons she recognizes and uses easily. For example, there is the lexicon of the fairy tale, the lexicon of a scolding by a parent, the lexicon of hanging out with friends, the lexicon of a schoolroom lesson, the lexicon of a TV host show, the lexicon of a ghost story, or the lexicon of a commercial, to name but a few. They are vividly distinct from one another.

Give your child a simple narrative sentence such as, "The boy met the girl in the hall." Ask her to choose one of the lexicons (without revealing the choice), and to rewrite and elaborate the simple sentence in new linguistic garb. For example, "Here it is! New! Factory to you! Wear Frizzo to school and see how quickly that girl will find *you* in the hall! Hurry! Don't miss out!" or, "Once upon a time, a timid orphan boy, afraid of his teacher who seemed like a wicked witch, was walking down the hall to math class. All of a sudden a moving, glowing cloud appeared, walking toward him. He looked around quickly to see whether the other kids had noticed, but they all kept right on walking . . ." Have your child read her offering aloud to see whether you can identify the lexicon.

Gifted, Precocious, or Just Plain Smart

- factual
- aesthetic
- imaginary

1. An intelligent fourth grader is old enough to begin a serious independent investigation. If your child is so inclined, he should be encouraged to choose a field, a topic, or a concept to pursue in whatever way matches his intellectual appetite. With any luck at all, the end product will be a portfolio, exhibit, report, or presentation that everyone can enjoy. Collecting solid factual information leads to strong conceptual foundations. I am told that over the front door to the Harvard Medical School is this quotation from Louis Pasteur: "Chance favors the prepared mind."

2. Together with your child, compile a list of ultimates: the noisiest, the zaniest, the most symmetrical, etc. Let her imagination soar. Then ask your child to choose one ultimate and find five contenders for that designation. She may write about them in prose or poetry, draw them, or create models.

3. Fourth graders sometimes have trouble remembering their manners and behaving in considerate ways. Humor is a great reminder. Ask your child to list five polite behaviors. Then ask him to make up skits depicting violations of those manners. Spoofing inconsiderate behavior actually underlines the more appropriate approach.

AFTERWORD

This book started in the kitchen with the Sprawler, the Compartmentalizer, the Inventor, the Whipper-Upper, and the Flash-in-the-Pan. Then there were the juvenile eaters: the Saver, the Devourer, the Musher, the Separator, and the Picker. Let's go back to the kitchen on a weekend early morning.

My healthy, lean husband, proud possessor of the lowest cholesterol levels in the family, likes to breakfast on eggs, sausages or bacon, buttered toast with jam, and strong black coffee. He anticipates the pleasure, savors every bite, and feels satisfied at the end. He's a scrambler.

I like two big glasses of juice, a bowl of dry cereal (no sugar) with low-fat milk, and hot tea. I'm a pourer.

My best friend has a glass of milk and a peanut butter and raspberry jam sandwich on whole wheat bread. She's a spreader.

Our son is B.D.—breakfast disabled. With half a glass of juice on the run, he's out the door. He's an avoider who eats a huge lunch.

So, there's something called breakfast (or something called school). Four people agree on the importance of food, all of them want to be nourished, care about their overall well-being, but are totally different in their approaches. The same is true of learners.

Of course, there are times when everyone must eat (or learn) the same thing in the same way. But when we can whet the learner's appetite by factoring in his or her learning patterns, we set the scene for good digestion.

With the tips and activities in this book, you're now prepared to set an inviting table for your child, creating opportunities for sharing and long-term nourishment.

Food for thought.

Bon appétit!

DOES IT ALL ADD UP: MYTH, MONSTER, OR MONOGRAM?[1]

"It all adds up. You wait and see. He's got it, all right." I couldn't tell whether the rasp in the teacher's voice was from threat or emphasis. I was there to visit her second-grade classroom, observing a little sinner named Carlo. The "it" he supposedly had was ADD—Attention Deficit Disorder, now renamed ADHD—Attention Deficit Hyperactivity Disorder.

Most classrooms I visit are lovely, but here the teacher stood in front of eighteen seated second graders and described phonics. The children were to listen to a stream of words about vowel teams.

Carlo turned himself sideways. His head was tipped up, and his gaze remained fixed through the thirty-minute lesson. When the group was dismissed, the teacher said, "What did I tell you? ADD. I read all about it in a magazine. That boy didn't listen to a word I said."

Later, I saw Carlo in the hall. "Tell me," I asked, "do you remember what you were thinking about back there in the phonics lesson?"

---

[1]©Copyright PLV 1991–92. Originally published in *Priscilla's Column,* by the New York Orton Dyslexia Society.

"Sure," he said. "Didn't you see? There was this sunbeam coming in the window, and inside it were all these little dust particles. They were kind of dancing—and rotating—the same pattern over and over. Then, I started wondering whether all the air in the room had the same kind of dust particles. Maybe the particles in the sunbeam moved because they were extra warm, or maybe they all moved at the same speed because they were dust. I don't know. Do you?"

No. I didn't know that, but I did know that this boy could focus and sustain his attention. And while I am semiglad his teacher had heard of ADD (she hadn't caught up with ADHD), I weep for the children being labeled with this buzz word by well-intentioned, uninformed people who are unqualified to make the diagnosis. Harm comes to the misdiagnosed; genuine need is pooh-poohed by crying wolf.

A second-grade boy who decides to study dust particles because he is bored by the lesson must not be labeled ADHD simply because his teacher likes children who maintain eye contact. Nor should normally active children be medicated because fate landed them under the control of Ms. Sitstillanlissen. And compassion belongs to the nonhyperactive ADD child whose pliant behavior camouflages scattered thinking.

When noted speakers at serious conferences ask whether ADD/ADHD is a myth, a monster, or a monogram, we all need to find bedrock. Within the confines of a short article, here is wisdom distilled from five physicians on six aspects of this chimera.

Caution. ADD and ADHD are medical terms referring to collections of symptoms. The diagnosis may be made only by a medical doctor, who, in turn, is bound by the constraints of The Diagnostic and Statistical Manual of Mental Disorders (commonly known as DSM-IV). The physician must see at least eight out of fourteen possible symptoms—such as impulsivity, restlessness, fidgety behavior, and poor concentration that must have been active for at least six months—and onset must have occurred before age seven. The physician may then decide to prescribe medication.

Diagnosis. Sylvia O. Richardson, M.D., says that ADD presents a very difficult problem in differential diagnosis. Accuracy does not come from the safe distance of an armchair, and firsthand knowledge of the child is required to rule out 1) a receptive language disorder, 2) high intensity temperamental attributes, and 3) what she calls hyper-*re*activity to stress.

Martha B. Denckla, M.D., uses the acronym ISIS in discussing attention. The letters stand for Initiate (can the kid get going?), Sustain (can the kid hang with the topic?), Inhibit (can the kid screen out internal or external distractions?), and Shift (can the kid break off and refocus?). These four capacities are present in most normal children and compromised in children with ADD or ADHD. Dr. Denckla also suggests that the letters should sometimes stand for Attentional Distribution Difference, to which I would add Attention Distribution Disobedience. Witness Carlo, the dust particle deviant.

Disguise. Larry Silver, M.D., makes the point that clinical depression in childhood is underestimated and under-recorded. Many of its symptoms—like those of anxiety—mimic those of ADD, leading to misdiagnosis. At a 1989 CHADD (Children and Adults with Attention-Deficit/Hyperactivity Disorder) conference, Dr. Silver urged increased vigilance for—and accurate diagnosis of—childhood depression. As is true of ADD/ADHD, this diagnosis—a medical prerogative—is not to be made by educators or parents.

LIBERATE YOUR CHILD'S LEARNING PATTERNS

Labels. Edward Hallowell, M.D., says that when terminology becomes cliché, people begin to disparage the underlying notion as well as the term itself. The results, in this instance, can be withdrawal of credibility from the concept of ADD, leaving genuinely afflicted students marooned in skepticism of the problem, presumption of bad attitude, attribution of low ability, withdrawal of help, and evaporation of helpful strategies.

Prescription. Robert Seaver, M.D., stresses the importance of accurate diagnosis—ruling out masqueraders mentioned above—followed by careful monitoring of dosage when medication is prescribed. Adjustment based on careful record keeping and enlightened observation underlie the required sensitive balance. The adults in the child's life need to be reminded of behaviors to watch for and have standardized assessment forms on which to record their impressions. The physician fine-tunes accordingly. The family, school, and physician must work in trustful common purpose. Sad to say, I hear increasing numbers of horror stories of courses of medication monitored only at six-month or one-year intervals.

In cases of genuine need, the medication—working through the arousal system—may free the student to concentrate and learn. Previous concerns over whether medication would cause generalized drug dependence or inhibition of growth appear unfounded.

Testing. Faith Howland, educational consultant, says "Help! I wish people would stop trying to use a WISC [Wechsler Intelligence Scale for Children, a widely used battery of tests] to diagnose ADD/ADHD. It was not designed to perform this task. A parent called me the other day to say 'Someone at the school said Tommy was ADD, so I had him tested with this IQ test, and he's not. So now what do I do?'"

DOES IT ALL ADD UP: MYTH, MONSTER, OR MONOGRAM?

School and Home. Is overdiagnosis a problem? When forty students in a school of four hundred are diagnosed ADD/ADHD in one year—and when the year before the number had been twelve—I worry.

Is the label misused? A parent who had been yearning for an instant fix to a complicated set of learning problems called me last week, saying, "Graham's been diagnosed. So nothing's his fault. He can take a pill and change schools."

A seemingly competent child with an undiagnosed language disability began to falter in third grade, where the language demands increase in rate, volume, and complexity. He needed to develop nature's own pathways to order, and verbal brakes on impulsivity: the language of space and time. His mother called and said, "I'm canceling out that language therapy. I know now. He's ADD. I saw it on the evening news."

As responsible adults, parents, educators, and physicians need to sharpen collective observational skills, find diagnostic bedrock, and fuel our combined index of suspicion with strong injections of common sense. In thinking about real live children and situations we actually know, we need to ask whether ADD/ADHD is the emperor's new clothes of nomenclature. We must ask how and whether it all ADDs up.

DOLCH SIGHT WORD LIST

Created by the late Edward Dolch of the University of Chicago, these 220 words are frequently seen in children's books and in everyday reading. They are called sight words because many of them cannot be learned through phonics or the use of pictures, and therefore must be recognized upon seeing them.

The words are presented in a random sequence instead of alphabetically because the purpose of using this word list with your child is true recognition, not memorization of sequence.

been	could	found	now	yellow
about	ran	big	gave	were
give	well	this	no	which
know	not	put	it	those
because	am	me	live	these
he	came	will	help	to
be	one	old	have	went
may	thank	keep	some	better
when	like	tell	every	them
new	go	has	with	or
my	sit	said	wash	that

open	can	must	call	jump
myself	your	three	got	best
long	him	pretty	far	grow
its	cold	ask	just	all
how	before	as	she	so
much	would	ride	both	five
I	only	here	by	write
and	is	green	want	make
again	ate	first	read	soon
a	seven	think	once	out
down	fall	red	work	fast
pull	eat	what	walk	blue
fly	see	round	use	from
please	brown	drink	always	if
hot	they	pick	was	after
six	light	today	many	under
shall	sing	draw	saw	but
going	black	own	for	her
off	hurt	made	are	around
ten	come	why	never	show
done	get	over	look	wish
run	good	had	kind	does
white	us	up	there	don't
stop	goes	take	two	at
in	our	sleep	too	who
clean	on	buy	do	did
upon	then	full	yes	play
his	warm	into	an	start
bring	eight	together	laugh	the
say	their	any	hold	right
funny	carry	we	cut	four
were	let	of	very	away
small	find	you	little	try

RESOURCES

Following are some resources that will provide additional information to help you further explore the topics discussed in this book.

---

www.priscillavail.com

Provides information about all of Priscilla L. Vail's books, as well as articles and additional resources on topics discussed in *Liberate Your Child's Learning Patterns.*

The following organizations provide additional information regarding topics discussed in this book:

The International Dyslexia Association

Chester Building, Suite 382

8600 LaSalle Road

Baltimore, MD 21286-2044

This organization brings together physicians, researchers, educators, and parents and offers excellent publications and conferences open to any interested participant.

Educators Publishing Service
31 Smith Place
Cambridge, MA 02138

This reliable publisher offers materials originally designed for dyslexics which work magnificently in regular classrooms. The descriptions and age/grade levels in their cataloges are scrupulously fair.

Modern Learning Press/Programs for Education
Box 167
Rosemont, NJ 08556
1-800-627-5867

This excellent publishing house offers a wide variety of books, classroom materials, videos, and art reproductions for educators and parents. It is a welcome resource.

The following books and/or authors were mentioned in *Liberate Your Child's Learning Patterns:*

Gardner, Howard. *Frames of Mind: The Theory of Multiple Intelligences.* New York: Basic Books, 1984. In this barrier-breaking book, Gardner expands the number and precision of the lenses through which we assess intelligence and recognize the potential in the children among us.

——— *The Unschooled Mind: How Children Think and How Schools Should Teach.* New York: Basic Books, 1992. Gardner gives us an insightful tour of the mind of the five-year-old thinker alive in all of us, and suggests ways to help learners move beyond that primitive level to genuine understanding.

RESOURCES

Hoban, Russell. *How Tom Beat Captain Najork and His Hired Sportsmen.* New York: Macmillan, 1974. This amusing and delightfully illustrated tale is meat and drink to fourth graders.

Koch, Kenneth. *Wishes, Lies, and Dreams: Teaching Children to Write Poetry.* New York: HarperCollins, 2000. This book of exercises on exploring poetry has helped thousands of children (and adults) discover an interior poet never before recognized or encouraged to speak.

Saint-Exupéry, Antoine de. *The Little Prince.* New York: Harcourt, Brace & World, 1941.

Traub, Nina. *Recipe for Reading.* Cambridge, MA: Educators Publishing Service, 2000. This volume of methods and materials, based on Orton-Gillingham principles, is a user-friendly companion for classroom teachers and parents.